Like Son, Like Father

Healing the Father–Son Wound in Men's Lives

Like Son, Like Father

Healing the Father–Son Wound in Men's Lives

Gregory Max Vogt, Ph.D.
and
Stephen T. Sirridge, Ph.D.

Plenum Press • New York and London

Library of Congress Cataloging-in-Publication Data

Vogt, Gregory Max.
Like son, like father : healing the father-son wound in men's lives / Gregory Max Vogt and Stephen T. Sirridge.
p. cm.
Includes bibliographical references and index.
ISBN 0-306-43970-0
1. Fathers--Psychology. 2. Fathers and sons. I. Sirridge, Stephen T. II. Title.
HQ756.V64 1991
306.874'2--dc20 91-20164
CIP

ISBN 0-306-43970-0

Plenum Press is a division of Plenum Publishing Corporation
233 Spring Street, New York, N.Y. 10013

Printed in the United States of America

This book is for Max and Lance.

—GMV

To William Thomas and Nathaniel Thomas,
father and son. —STS

Contents

Chapter 1

Men, We Invite You to Change

A new kind of man is emerging in our time. He is a man with a strong sense of masculinity, yet he is breaking through limiting stereotypical roles. He is rediscovering the meaning and joys of being a man, a father, and a son. He is unearthing the sleeping being within him, a creative, zestful, emotionally connected man. He is productive in the work world, yet involved in raising his family, available to his children and to his partner. He is finding new possibilities of friendships with other men which deepen and strengthen the bonds he already has with them. He is finding the value of equal and enduring relationships with women. He is sexual and passionate, yet nurturing and empathetic with others. He is learning how to play, how to enjoy himself, and yet to be highly dedicated and efficient in his work. He is reconnecting with his family of origin and is deeply interested in the history of the generations before him. He does his best to promote and remain in contact with men of his own age as well as older and younger men. He is giving of his time and energy to the development of younger men and seeking the advice and help of older men.

He is a man with skills, potential, commitment, and spiritual values. These new men of the nineties are beginning to appear in ever-increasing numbers. They are challenging the idea that men must conform to the definitions of men that they were scripted to follow. They are refusing to resign themselves to the roles or expectations that have been accepted by many men in American society.

Unfortunately, many men describe lives of isolation, addictions, and lack of intimacy with both men and women. The incidence of major depression has increased in males, young and old. Men, on the average, live almost ten years less than women in this country. Men are addicted to alcohol and drugs at a ratio of four men for every one woman. All the major stress-related diseases leading to death show significantly higher rates for males. Men commit crimes of violence much more often than women.

Yet, all over the country, men are doing something about these problems. They are working for changes in their relationships with each other and with their families. A rapidly growing number of men are ready to break their isolation and increase their intimacy with other men and women. They want to build deep, enduring connections with others. They are working hard to find new meaning and enjoyment in their masculinity, and are finding new definitions of what it means to "be a man." They have a new commitment to satisfaction in all areas of their lives—at work, in their families, in friendships, and in their love relationships. We invite you to be a part of these changes and increase your own satisfaction with your life.

There is hope, and there are specific things you can do to achieve the goals that you want out of your relationships with other people and with yourself. We have written this book to give you resources that will not only promote your understanding of men and their relationships, but have immediate possibilities of helping you in all aspects of your inner and outer life. We have given attention to most of the major areas of men's lives, from work to love to play to addictions to the relationship with your family of origin. We want you to have a solid understanding of what has gone wrong and that you nonetheless have exactly what you need to work on "getting things right" for you in your relationships.

The book works in three ways. First, each chapter tackles a basic "area" of relationships with yourself or with others. We will give you a good, basic, working understanding of what difficulties can arise and how they come about for each man. Second, we provide immediately usable exercises and challenges for men that each of you can use either individually or in groups to affect change—more on this in a minute. Third, we give you additional resources you can consult to broaden and deepen your own work and connect with others who are committed to developing themselves. You can use any or all of these ways; they all offer approaches to broadening and deepening your relationships.

In each chapter we have included exercises for men. The exercises will be things to do sometimes by yourself, sometimes with one other person, and sometimes most appropriately in groups. There are no right or wrong answers to the questionnaires included nor is there a "right" way to use the exercises, except in a few cases. Try as many exercises and accept as many of the challenges they offer you as you can. Use our models and create your own. Some of the exercises or information can result in changes in men immediately. If you pay attention, you may notice some changes in yourself right away. Other changes can take longer—weeks, months, or even years. Some of the things we ask you to do may take a lifetime to take effect, because they will begin changes in basic patterns of relating to others that have been developed in your family and culture for many generations before you. We hope you believe, as we do, that having fuller, deeper relationships with other people is worth the effort, even if it is hard work.

Think, feel, sense in your body, be aware of yourself. These are the things that many men have forgotten how to do. This book will provide thought, feeling, sensations, and memory. We have written the book to be useful and hope it will become dog-eared as you refer back to it repeatedly in your own work on relationships with others and with yourself.

Now, let us start by talking more about "how men got this way." If you have a good idea of where you are coming from, you can have a better idea of what stops you, what blocks you from developing in ways you hope to go. One very key element in the formation of men's relationships is the relationship between son and father. The model of this relationship influences everything in a man's life, from the way he sees himself inside to the way he sees all other people, power, economics, politics, and even his vision of the natural world.

Some writers and thinkers have suggested that the woundedness that many men experience, their disenchantment, disillusionment, and alienation, is the result of many traditionally held masculine virtues or values, such as prowess, competition, victory, aggression, strength, directed, or linear, thinking. Such qualities, often referred to as "patriarchal" or as "qualities of the patriarchy," are viewed by these writers as hurtful, destructive, divisive, and hierarchical. This suggests not only that the traditional masculine qualities *per se* are called into doubt, but that in addition, by consequence, the traditional way of a father rearing a son is called into serious question.

Throughout this book we use the terms male and masculine, female and feminine. The way we are using these terms is as follows. *Male* and *female* refer to biological sex differences, to men and women. *Masculine* and *feminine* are qualities of gender that are not biological but defined by culture. In one culture, at one time, dressing in flamboyant and gaudy clothes may be seen as masculine; and at the same moment in history in another culture, as feminine. For the purposes of this book, we are using the term masculine as synonymous with strength, determination, straightforwardness, virility, courage, tenacity, and firmness. These qualities can just as well be found in women (perhaps in different forms than in men). This book, however, concentrates on men and their experience of masculinity.

Today, many boys are growing up without a model of masculinity. They are growing toward manhood without the presence of a father, either literally without a father—growing up in a single-parent family with mother only—or without the presence of a confident and emotionally available father. Many fathers today do not know what to do with their sons, and feel lost and frozen as fathers. Many factors have contributed to the sense of woundedness and alienation that men feel today—economic, social, cultural, and political factors all play a great part. However, a very major contributor to the sense of loss of the American man today is the result of a breakdown in the relationship between sons and fathers. Many sons today—this includes fathers, who are, of course, sons themselves—describe their experiences as that of betrayal and abandonment by their father. Many fathers describe that they don't know how to interact with their sons. Adolescents are floating aimlessly, middle-aged fathers are fighting addictions, older fathers and grandfathers are plagued by lethargy and disillusionment. Many men move through life disconnected from others like them. Their despair begins early in life with a vague sense of rootlessness and often ends in regret, lost opportunities, and loneliness. A noted family therapist, Augustus Napier, has written that

> a disproportionate number of males are rejected kids. Not only do boys feel abandoned by their preoccupied, psychologically distant fathers, but they are also subject to the anger of their unhappy mothers. There is a good deal of sociological evidence that points toward rejection being a central issue in males: from the higher incidence of alcoholism and substance abuse, to the much higher incidence of suicide, to men's general emotional isolation. (p. 194)

So how did we become "rejected kids"? What went wrong? Part of the answer lies in the changing American family. When forty percent of all marriages (and sixty percent of all second marriages!) fail, you know there are a number of boys and girls who live day to day without the physical presence of a father. Also, career demands pull fathers away during the bustle and activity of the week. Not only is the power and potency that dad brings to help order and discipline lost, but also that necessary balance of energy and perspective that mom and dad provide together. Sons are robbed of the opportunity of bumping into dad on the way to the next room, getting help for an algebra problem, or being tucked into bed. Boys learn that time with dad is at best scheduled and time-slotted, and revolves around a vacation-like weekend full of movies, pizza, expanded rules, and potato chips. Gone are quiet moments, daily routines, "regularity"—the sense of living together day after day in peace.

What is the legacy of this situation for the next generations? It creates a multigenerational problem of male isolation and disengagement. Unfortunately, a son grows up to be a father today with a sense that it is more "natural" to be "away" than to be present, an outsider looking in who is only dimly aware of the family closeness which eludes him.

Another answer for this estrangement which men feel is the continuous cultural bombardment of images which show a "real man" as one who is self-absorbed and a "rugged individualist." There is a great deal of attention paid to competition instead of cooperation. Competition is important, but as the highest value on the totem pole, it has the effect of utter isolation for the individual man.

A member of our men's group, George, recently noticed that he doesn't have any "real friends." All of the men he associates with are just that—associates. He believes that he "can't trust them" with information about himself, because they might be "potential competitors." He even noticed that he has been trying to get his "best friend" to invest in a deal he was negotiating. Fortunately, the other man said that he "would rather be a friend than lose one over a financial transaction." George realized he was "pissed off" that the other man wouldn't invest, but saw the wisdom in his decision to keep a limit and value the friendship more than making a few dollars. George notices, however, that he still doesn't trust his friend, and attributes it to the thinking that, "you just don't know when someone is going to end up being a competitor, and you just don't want the guy to end up with an edge."

American men are taught to value:

- competition over cooperation
- doing/performing over being and belonging
- efficiency over morals

- winning over enjoyment
- individual over the group
- blame over responsibility

Going it alone in search of external rewards is a value which supersedes belonging, enjoyment, and deep emotional connections. Cultural values deeply influence the way in which men attempt to feel good about themselves and the amount which they will invest in relationships, family, spiritual values, and self-awareness.

For boys who grew up in the families of the 1940s, 1950s, and 1960s, fathers were often physically absent or emotionally "just not there when they were there." Men were off at war, hiding behind newspapers, camped out in clubs or lodges, or tinkering alone in the family garage, and even drunk. The last few generations of men grew up without the "steady presence" of a father. When they later set up to play house, they found little to draw upon other than vapid television images, a fantasy of the ideal father: a lovable, dim-witted bungler, who always seemed to have a benevolent way of hanging around the house when a guy really needed him—Ozzie Nelson. Real-life fathers were phantoms or strangers returning from war, and even those sons who claim to have a relationship with dad are asking themselves if they have ever actually known him. Many of us say we are close to our fathers and upon reflection find little more in our connection with them beyond sports and the weather.

Over the past fifteen years of teaching and clinical practice, we have been listening to what men are saying about each other, to their befuddlement and frustration with themselves and other males. These are some of the things we have heard.

What do sons say about their fathers?

- humorless and unemotional
- bound to tradition
- rigid and conservative
- preoccupied
- distant and uninvolved
- close-minded and resistant to change
- obsessed with duty, honor, and money

What do fathers say about their sons?

- lack motivation and perserverance
- low frustration tolerance
- pursue the trivial and mundane
- no work ethic
- fail to take responsibility
- no appreciation for quality and tradition
- look for the easy way or clever angle
- lack respect and are usually ungrateful

Fathers and sons, after blaming and criticizing others, also talk about their own failures and doubts.

What do fathers say about themselves?

- We are not good at relationships, feelings, or closeness.
- No one wants our advice; why?
- We can't seem to contact our sons without being rejected.
- We wish we had our sons' respect.
- We wish we had more to give than money.
- We feel helpless in our silence and lack of options to connect with our sons.

What do sons say about themselves?

- Who needs fathers anyway? We will make it on our own.

- We feel like failures.
- We don't know how to please our fathers.
- How can we make our fathers proud of us?
- We just don't measure up to our own expectations or those of our fathers.
- We feel helpless in our silence and lack of options to connect with our fathers.

Something of a standoff, isn't it? When communication is so stagnated, so frozen between two parties, there will always be unresolved dilemmas. Some of the unresolved issues between sons and fathers that we often see include:

- Sons who are living up/down the expectations and reputations of their fathers.
- Sons and fathers with too little involvement with each other.
- Fathers repeating the patterns of detachment from the family and losing their connections to their sons.
- Fathers and sons feeling like they are failing to know each other.
- Fathers and sons feeling unappreciated and unrespected.
- Fathers and sons feeling the pain of isolation from each other and the lack of needed closeness.
- Fathers and sons finding too little common ground.
- Fathers and sons intolerant of each other's values and unique talents.
- Fathers and sons looking for escape in addictions.
- Fathers and sons struggling to find a place with each other within the family and within their peer groups.
- Fathers and sons attempting each in their own way to "make their mark on the world" and lacking confidence about where or how to do that.

How could fathers and sons be such strangers to each other? Part of the answer lies in the changes that have taken place in the workplace. As technology has pulled the father away to workplaces "on the other side of town," young boys have lost contact with dad. They have also stopped seeing other, older males in their lives, such as their father's co-workers, their grandfathers and uncles. It was considered an important ritual, in past times, for the father to pass his knowledge to his son of how to "make it" in the world and how to "make the world work" for himself. The son learned a skill and established a connection to his father in the world of men. Skill learning—such an important direct link between father and son—is almost completely lost in today's world. Similarly, much of what we do in the modern workplace is not visible activity. We sit in offices "shuffling electronic paper" (fax) and communicating with screens. There is a certain degree of "abstractness" about what many of us do.

SONS: "Daddy, what do you do at work?"
FATHERS: "I sell junk bonds;" "I handle underwriter's insurance;" "I diagnose schizophrenia."

How can you explain such concepts to a little boy? As far as that goes, how can we explain such concepts to ourselves? If you have a young son, or know a young boy, try an experiment. Talk to him about what you do and how you do it. Try to make it very clear and do your best to make certain he understands. Notice your own reactions as you make this explanation. Then, if it is possible, consider taking him to the place you work and showing him around. Show him exactly where you work and what you do. Even for those of us who work directly with our hands—carpenters, bricklayers, factory workers (if by the printing of this book, there are actually human beings working in factories), retail clerks—do our sons, or do we, really know why and for what purpose we are working? Do our sons see us at work? Did we see our fathers work?

When we lost the directness and concreteness of what we do, we also lost the sense of multigenerational linking. Today, father leaves for work and his eight-year-old son is not going to go by after school and wave at dad through the window; nor is grandfather going to "drop by the office" to see him. For most of us, work has created a geographical distance between home, work, and community/neighborhood. The father's father is no longer much involved in either his son's or his grandson's life. The grandson doesn't get much opportunity to see his father as a son.

Often we see young men walking around in the malls, their "home away from home," with no sense of a community of men. They are spending time only in the presence of other kids—bored, aimless, a sort of "homeless" people. Is it any wonder why males who spend time only with their peers carry a childhood masculinity based on being a boy? Father and son relationships have also been beset by outmoded and unchanging role options for masculinity. Betty Freidan wrote that men are "fellow victims suffering from an outmoded masculine mystique that made them feel unnecessarily inadequate where there were no more bears to kill" (Pittman, 1988, p. 40).

We have not found alternative ways of being that allow us to express our physical selves and provide a sense of adequacy and importance. Many men today run around the world shutting off their feelings and awareness of their bodies, locked into repetitive pursuits of "adequacy through domination" that drain away creativity and passion. Sons watch their fathers as they growl, stomp, dominate, and manipulate, attempting to find some alternative for "killing bears." The driven "let's close a big deal" man, the "macho man," the "breadwinner man of the fifties," the "mellow sixties man," the "sensitive seventies man," the "entrepreneurial or New Age eighties man"—all of these stereotyped models leave men feeling incomplete and unfulfilled. They don't really have to do with a living, breathing man, but are empty ideals.

The father, that guy with his humanity intact who is around the house, paying attention to his son, is the absolute best chance a boy has for growing up settled into himself. The father's physical presence is powerful. If a boy grows up touching a grown man's body, he can feel, sense, and experience things about a man: the strength of muscle tissue, the size and smell of his body, the sound of his heartbeat, the weight of dad's body as he pushes against him. This concrete sense comes out of a physical proximity to the father and other people and is essential to awareness of our humanity in flesh and blood. My own young son smells me after I work in the yard. He rushes up and "crushes" whatever part of me he can grab. He looks at me and shouts "Daddy!" making the fiercest face he can muster. He is working on knowing his own being, his physical and emotional body, through contact with me.

In the chapters that follow we have attempted to draw together a workable, concrete model for fathers and sons in their relationships with each other, and also for grown men in the community with other men. We encourage you to assess the status of your current relationship with your father or son as you have read this chapter. The intent is for you to identify areas of conflict or neglect and make more relevant the following chapters, which focus on "how things got that way" and "what can I do about it now?"

The first two chapters emphasize the father's presence

as the core experience needed by all males. In Chapter 2, "Motherbound Males," we discuss some problem areas for the son who gets caught too tightly in his bond with his mother and is not able to pull away and establish his unique, masculine self. We address the theme of male energy in the father and how his power is essential in drawing the son in a positive manner from his attachment to the "maternal orbit" and toward developing his sense of self as a male.

In Chapters 3 through 5, we have developed numerous metaphors for describing how the kinesthetic experience of masculinity is passed from the body of the adult male to the young boy. The father challenges, shields, nurtures, and protects, and he offers a lifelong sense of mystery and awe which the son will only come to know when he himself becomes one of "The Fathers."

The middle chapters (6–9) trace a man as he exists in adulthood "in the world." Central experiences such as work, friendships, and relationships with women are discussed. An ever-present theme in these chapters is how men operate on the basis of their early models in the son and father relationship, the impact of the early experience. Men who have had a limited, restricted, "stereotypical" experience of masculinity will have a tough time getting much satisfaction in the world. With the repression of creativity and flexibility, many men turn to the desperate use of mind-altering substances or other addictive activities to try to escape a prison of joylessness. We speak of how much is lost by men caught up in the addictive process and the challenge of living with the natural rhythms of the body. A final group of chapters (10–12) addresses the process of healing, reconciliation, and opportunities for renewed growth. The wounded man must first make his own personal peace, requiring steps which we suggest. Then he can transfer this knowledge into his relationships with others. A chapter on "mentoring" discusses the extremely important role of the "wise men," the older men, for us as we move through life. Mentors seem to appreciate aspects of us that our families will not or cannot see.

The book closes with the "Father's Blessing," a sort of benediction to the relationship of father and son that we see as so vital and basic to the spiritual life of all men. Our hope is that the future holds possibilities of greater and more positive connections between the generations, enriched friendships, and a sense of "being at home" in the community of men, and that this book may in its own way contribute to your finding that home.

Chapter 2

Motherbound Males

The Hatchers came in for family therapy with me. Don Hatcher is twenty-five years old and is just now thinking about moving away from home; maybe he's going to move out of the house pretty soon, he tells his buddies. The "boy's" father, Ted, is an alcoholic and is very distant and cold with Don. Ted works long hours as an engineer, and is often out of town. He is an excellent "provider," financially speaking, for the family. Ted is, however, solicitous with his wife, Theresa. He buys her gifts on his business trips, takes her to Paris with him twice a year, is very courteous with her most of the time, and rarely yells at her—except in disagreement about Don. Ted calls his own mother weekly. The subject of their discussion usually centers on "what to do about Don." Theresa is very warm, understanding, and supportive with Don, continuously trying to help her son figure out what he is going to do with his life, how to date, how to be with girls, what kind of social life he should have, how to get along with his father, and how to avoid abusing alcohol and drugs. Don is starting to experiment pretty widely with drugs and is moody and sullen most of the time. Theresa is really trying hard to counsel him against drugs or alcohol, and to help him get a job or get motivated to go back to college. Don often sleeps till noon. When he gets up, Theresa fixes his lunch. Don went away to college for one year and did terribly. One of the things he said about that time is that he missed his mom a lot. He knew that this was wrong for a guy his age, that he should be moving on, but it was still true. He missed his mother's support, having her around all the time to call or go over and visit. Even while he was away in college she did his laundry and cooked up all kinds of little "care packages" for him—muffins, trail mix, cookies, banana nut bread, and the like—and would send this sustenant knapsack for him to survive out in the world.

Don sat looking at his parents while they described him. He looked like he was amused by this portrait of himself and his family. Then he spoke up. Don told me, laughing, that it was really like he and his mother were married and that the father was just somebody who was there like a boarder, another—but insignificant—man in the house. He said, "Of course, there's no sex, but then again, there's none between the two of them either, is there?" He smiled widely with this clever comment. He caught a stinging glare from his father, which had little effect. Ted flushed, embarrassed, and hissed at Don between his teeth, "That's none of your business. You don't know anything about it." "Yes, he does," spoke Theresa sheepishly, trying not to look at either of the men. Don crossed his arms and looked smug.

The connection, or the emotional "marriage" between Theresa and Don, effectively placed Ted on the outside as the "third wheel." And most unfortunately for Don, all of the energy he needed to gather to make his own life work was diverted into his absorbingly close relationship with his mother. Boys get bound, or even "stuck," to their mothers frequently in our culture, some in a more overt fashion, like Don, but many in less obvious ways, like Ted with his mother. There is a certain emotional connection that takes place if a boy grows up depending on his mother too much. There is also a "stuckness" to mom as the boy grows into manhood—and she is the woman he is most closely connected to—if he hasn't somehow severed that intense, preoccupying connection.

Jack, a forty-two-year-old male nurse, was seen for therapy at a hospital outpatient office for his second episode of severe depression. He was brought to the clinic by his sixty-seven-year-old mother because he stopped working and was having trouble sleeping, and feeling hopeless about life. Jack has always been close to his parents and lived at home. His father died when he was twenty-six, leaving Jack as the sole companion to his mother these past sixteen years. He has had a few dates, but no relationship lasted more than a couple of months. He has changed job locations numerous times, interspersed with periods of apathy and listlessness. His mother, who has a heart condition, has told him that she will die if he moves out, though he yearns for a life of his own. He is not sure what life would be like without the steady presence of his mother.

As exemplified in Jack's life, there can begin to be a kind of sacramental element to mother and son's relationship, a bonding together which ends in a sacrifice of independence by both of them. They begin to appear as if they had taken vows to remain stuck to each other. A lot of times you will see middle-aged or older men who have continued to live with their mothers. They become sort of an old couple together, since old age seems to have a neutralizing effect on their age difference. The man really never finds his place outside of that relationship. They become an inseparable couple and psychologically marry each other.

These are the most blatant examples of what happens when males are bound to their mothers, the obvious feature being that they either live with them or spend a lot of time moving back and forth between houses. These sons can even be married, yet the wife senses that her husband's primary allegiance is always toward his mother. We have heard cases of men who will use their spare time to do errands and work for their mothers before they will even do such things in their own home. They will go over and mow the mother's lawn, and adjust the plumbing and fix the roof, yet those very same items within their own homes sometimes go untouched because of their allegiance, the belief that they still owe things to mother first.

How does this allegiance develop between mother and boy? One contributing factor has to do with the nature of the connection between the spouses—the original parents. In these families, the relationship between the mother and the father as husband and wife is not particularly strong, and either the mother's allegiance is greater to her mother or her father, or the father's to his mother. Somehow one or both of the spouses has not experienced the model of a close marriage and thus is unable to make the depth of commitment to his or her own spouse.

When the child enters the picture, it is easy for one or both parents—in this case we are concentrating on the mother—to continue a pattern that was already begun in her family of origin. From her childhood, she had felt a stronger bond between her mother and her than what was between her two parents. This provides the underpinnings for a strong dialogue between the mother and child with the father being excluded. Evidence of this pattern starts even before the child is born—when there is a weak, fragile bond between the parents. In such cases the couple may share interests but develop few strong ties of closeness.

An example of a child-focused marriage is demonstrated in the family of Linda. Linda, a single mother, brought her fifteen-year-old son, Sean, to counseling in response to continual outbursts of anger and property destruction by the boy. A look at his records showed previous contact with a psychologist when Sean was four and a half years old, with the psychologist recommending that Linda shift some of her attention away from Sean to avoid overprotectiveness and overconcern, that Sean might develop more normally if encouraged to greater independence, and that Linda consider having more of a life of her own, for the boy's sake and for hers. Linda disregarded the advice and, if anything, spent more time and attention on Sean, who continued to be a problem, with his mother continuously rescuing him whenever he got in trouble. He had a three-week hospitalization after psychiatric referral from juvenile court; he had destroyed property in a neighbor's house while the neighbor was out of town and had been arrested.

Linda married Robert when Sean was ten years old. Robert complained frequently that Linda paid more attention to Sean than to him, and seemed to have little interest in his stepson. The family was referred to me for family therapy after Sean's hospitalization. When the three came in for therapy, Robert and Linda were barely speaking to each other, enjoyed few interests in common, and saw their marriage as very "detached," though they admitted they had been "madly in love" when they first met and then married. Robert claimed the reason that the marriage was failing was because "Sean and Linda are glued together—there is no room at all for me." Linda claimed it was because "Robert won't accept Sean." Sean refused to talk at all, but spent most of the session looking down at his shoes, glaring or snorting disapproval at Robert and me, or asking his mother, frequently, if he could leave, "step out for a smoke," go to the bathroom, or if he had to answer anything I asked him.

A new son (or daughter), as in the case of Sean and his parents, pulls at any weak link in a marriage and settles in a spot between the parents. Dad, often excluded from early caretaking, begins a shift away from family to work or friends, or in some cases, awaits the birth of a second child that can be his favorite. Another thing that creates friction in the parents' relationship is a kind of natural consequence of the passing years. Women often complain about how their husbands have changed over time. We hear frequently that when a woman first meets her husband, he has a sort of youthful male exuberance, a playfulness, a kind of joy about him, and a lot of sexual energy. She develops a relationship with this boy—he is a boy in some ways when they meet—and then as time goes on and the husband becomes, frequently, more involved in his career or other events in the world, some of his boyish exuberance, fun, and excitement about the world begins to wane. He becomes more connected to his job, to money-making, to "prestige," and to his business associates.

When a son comes along, sometimes a mother sees in the son a kind of new spiritual marriage. Once again she can see, in her son, a youthful male exuberance, this brash, loud excitement in the young boy which had excited her when she met her husband. This playfulness no longer seems available in the husband, but is present in her young son. There is a draw toward that excitement and newness in the young boy. In the Hatcher family, Theresa had lost interest in Ted, with his long trips and his focus on his own mother. Don seemed so appreciative, and easy to please, that it felt natural to be excited about being with him.

This is an interesting and often repeated scenario, one that we think served as the basis of the family dynamics in the book and movie *Ordinary People.* The father is portrayed as a serious, passive, laid-back lawyer type. We soon learn that the mother had actually been carrying on a kind of love relationship with the oldest son, who had exhibited a strong exuberance and zest for life. In fact, the boy's name was Buck. When you stood the son alongside the father, it was easy to see who would elicit more excitement in the mother. Buck's hopefulness, his dreams, his passions, his "physicalness," his playfulness, and his boyishness worked together to attract her. And, of course, she wasn't able to relate to her second son because he mirrored the father in a much greater way. He was introverted, serious, and quiet. His passions did not reveal themselves in the ways that the older son's did. What became problematic in the mother–son relationship was the fact that this boyish person she loved—Buck—died, and she was left not only with that terrible loss but with two other men who were so different from the boy who had been her passion.

Art mirrors much of life in that we often see a strong love between two people fade and dwindle to nothing, with each person looking for more exciting replacements. Why is it that sometimes that connection between parents unravels? In some cases the bond is absent to begin with. In other cases, there is a good chemistry that existed between the two at first that somehow was lost; and now the son has become a kind of reincarnation of something that the mother lost when her husband changed. In a way, the boy died and a particular type of father—a staid, righteous, rigid old man—was born.

In the recent press, numerous articles have surfaced about different-aged people connecting with each other and finding each other attractive: older men and young women, older women and younger men. One of the reasons older women prefer younger men is that men their own age are not as interesting; they are not as much fun or as passionate as the younger men. The older man may be searching out a younger woman to rekindle the youthful zest and brashness of his own adolescence, or to find liveliness and passion in another person that he has trouble finding in himself. Young women who go after older men are often attracted to their stability and even-temperedness and patience, like one might expect in a father.

Many young men voice their interest in older women for some of the same reasons that young men are interested in older men: the stability, even-temperedness and patience, so-called fatherly qualities. They have made it, they are secure in themselves, they are grounded, solid, and experienced. The older woman knows about life and is therefore a good instructor about the world. Some of the kinds of things that a boy might desire in a mother—or even more likely, that he might desire in a father—are achieved in these relationships. One might even ask if the younger men are interested in older women because of a fantasy that they might be able to have in a woman both a replacement for their mother and for their father. They may be looking for nurturance and assurance as well as protection and guidance.

In Don Hatcher's family, we see that Don circles in his mother's orbit in a very literal way. He stays very "tight" with his mother, even to the point that we wonder if he will ever be able to move out of the house or have a sense of independence. This is one family scenario that produces underfunctioning males, who never really seem to get a life of their own, but stay boys or sons on into their later years. Another, more frequently seen pattern is males who still emotionally "live at home with mother," though they may be out on their own. Their general approach to the world, the way they carry themselves, and their attitude is one of not having carved out a separate identity for themselves.

These men may have a certain gentleness about them, tenderness, good listening skills, sensitivity to feelings, sensitivity to what women need and what they want—and a willingness, sometimes an absolute drive to please women. However, despite this drive, they may be very passive sexually, and they will often collapse under direct criticism, confrontation, or expression of strong emotion by a potent woman. Even though they may have developed their ability to be in relationships with women to a greater extent than many men, it seems they have lost some of their own sense of self in the process. Something is missing inside, specifically an inner sense of self-confidence and independence. These men hang their identity on the definitions of them given by women.

One woman, Tina, describes the situation like this:

> My boyfriend, Jack, is a very nice man. He is a brilliant conversationalist, a great companion, and we have a lot of interests in common. He is great to be around—as long as I am feeling happy and content. The minute I am depressed, stressed out, and anxious about something, or have the tiniest criticism of him, he just seems to disappear into a black hole, into a deep despair. It's hard for me to be natural about my emotions around him, unless I am feeling happy or excited.

A strong, self-confident father can be a model for a son of both sensitivity to other people and autonomy, that is, a sense of security in one's own value. And he can help guide his son to finding these qualities in himself. A mature man is able to be boyish, excited, sexually and romantically involved without being obsequious, sappy, or compulsive about pleasing women.

There is an old-fashioned expression that was used a lot in the 1950s. It's not heard much now, but it is relevant to this discussion. We used to refer to boys who spent too much time at home when they were big enough to be out with the guys (e.g., in adolescence or beyond) as "tied to the mother's apron strings." Symbolically, the apron has two basic images. First, it is connected with food, feeding, and the kitchen. So the apron is a kind of placenta upon which the boy can rest his head, and there is a sort of membranous infusion of feeding that takes place. The string of the apron is the umbilical cord. The boy is still being dragged around by or is following the umbilical cord waiting to be intravenously fed, and to have the supplies delivered to him that he still believes he needs so desperately from his mother.

One of the complaints of the women's movement is that men don't seem to be able to provide their own food or other "supplies." A woman goes to a man's house to visit him and he will only have a pizza and beer in the refrigerator. She will start filling the refrigerator with vegetables and cheese and other supplies. There is something basic missing in a lot of men who are still waiting for the infusion of mother's sustaining nourishment on into their forties. Some single men still go over to mom's house for dinner on Monday night. She still does the wash. They go back to their own homes for the rest of the week and eat out every night. This is still a manifestation of the same tendency: waiting for someone else to deliver the supplies, rather than taking charge and just "bringing home the bacon"—the traditional father's chore—and then simply fixing it with no fuss or without waiting for "mom to come home." But these types of males often are very macho and marry traditionalist women to take over the wash and fix them a glass of milk before bed.

Tied to the mother's apron strings, these boys just trail their mothers around the house. The word "motherbound" suggests the image of a boy swaddled, like we see in traditional societies where the cloth is wrapped around the mother and baby. Some men still seem to be waiting to be picked up and swaddled to mother.

The mother-binding scenario has two basic features. First, the mother seems to have a need to keep her son close, which can become a mutual kind of need over time. The son also feels a strong need for his mother. Second, the absence of the father is often a factor, since there is no force which is strong enough or insistent enough to pull the son out into the world, to cut loose the apron strings, and move the kid out of the kitchen and into the workshop. The cutting of the apron strings is a kind of emotional severing. One of the things we see with motherbound males is that they avoid being directly confrontational with anyone. They may be bitchy, they may be grouchy, but they don't confront directly. They do everything they can to prevent that severing from the mother, that cutting free of the mother's influence, and growing up to be autonomous.

An illustration of a motherbound male very much in need of something from his father is portrayed by the son of a family who came to consult with me—the Samuelsons, a mother, father, and twenty-year-old son. The son was in college, and was not doing well; in fact, he had hidden this secret about his school problems from both of his parents. This was the big crisis. Interestingly enough, it was much more of a crisis for the mother than for the father. Anyway, they all came in for a session. As I looked at the son, I was aware of his background of being a good student, a football player, and now a fraternity man. Here was a boy who was attempting to look like a man, but was very soft inside. He could probably be physical but he was essentially soft and passive inside with the outer covering of a strong male. This observation became clear as I became aware that a more intense relationship existed between the son and the mother than between the son and the father. The father dressed as a very successful businessman, and I would classify his dress as "slick."

What I saw here was that the father's big concern—really his only concern—was that the son be able to "get his act together." His college performance was "really going to have an effect on him." If he had the grades to go to law school, he could make good money. If he was smart, he would adopt some businesslike habits which would get his life in order, help him to plan his time better, and look the part of someone who was going to be a success in life.

What this father was offering his son was a business model solution to a life problem. The mother offered herself—she wanted to be there for him more, and she thought he needed better monitoring from home. This was her explanation for why he was not succeeding in college. The reason he needed to be monitored was that he had not been sharing what had been going on at college with her; what needed to happen now was for him to come home twice a week from college in order to have more face-to-face contact with his parents. She felt that this communication—especially with her advice, and the father's business views—would lead to a success for their son.

Despite any attempt on my part to suggest to each member of the family that the son might need to have a chance to succeed or fail on his own account, the emphasis was always drawn back during this session to the parents' involvement with their son's every decision. The family was convinced, or at least the parents were, that the kid couldn't make it without mom and dad's marshalling, each in his or her own way. The mother continuously wanted to focus on the young man's bond with her and the father. The father wanted the kid to "get discipline" like he had, the way he had control of himself, and "get things straight." The mother wanted to tie the kid back; that is, what he really needed was more supplies from home. He needed to get back to the apron more. The father's vision was that what he really needed to do was to work more on the shell, the outer way of presenting himself, even down to the style of "dressing for success." That would do it. The father said, "While we are here, why don't I say something that has been bugging me? Do you think that sometime when you come home to visit us—at least for your mother's sake—you could wear one of your $150 sweaters?"

Mother and father each offer unhelpful solutions for their son. The potential strategies do not facilitate the son's separating and building personal responsibility. Mother offers monitoring typical of a junior high school student and father offers sterile advice which he hopes will transfer from business to academics. We mention this case because each parent, though well-intentioned, is caught in a stereotypic stance with regard to the son's dilemma. Any funding for this young man's schooling should be tied to his improvement as a student, and it should be his own responsibility whether to pass or fail. Each parent should only offer help that the son asks for and is willing and motivated to implement. This solution goes quite a bit beyond mother's over-involvement or father's attempts to give a solution "from on high." Our position encourages the son to face his own life or develop his own ways to operate in life, with the caring, but not rescuing or preaching, support of his parents.

A member of one of our men's groups, Larry, a man in his late forties, decided to do something different with his family of origin. Throughout his adult life until recently, whenever arrangements were made about visits, holidays, and the like, he talked only with his mother on the telephone about arranging such get-togethers. Recently, Larry decided to put more attention to establishing a relationship with his father. So, for the first time in his life, he wrote a letter addressed just to his father. He immediately felt a combination of emotions. He was relieved and felt liberated, but at the same time terrified about "leaving his mother out." He even had the thought that she might "have a heart attack" or feel "terribly depressed" as a result of his action. It was amazing that he had never written to his father in over twenty years, and now he was writing him one letter, a newsy letter at that. But he was also leaving his mother out of this moment and was just focusing on sending something to his father.

It took about two days for the letter to get there, and his father read the letter on the evening of the day it arrived. The next day, when the father was away, the mother called the son to see if "everything was ok," to see if he was sick or if he was having some sort of problem. This was an indication to him that she was beginning to feel his move to become a little separate from her and closer to his father. She reacted to it. She wanted him back. She didn't really want him to be closely connected to his father. But what she said out loud was the very opposite. She said, "I think it is wonderful that you are deciding to write and talk to your father now." But she still called and nonetheless said, "What's going on, are you sick?"

What is being said on the overt level is that relationships are encouraged among all parties. Yet there is a subtle and sometimes not so subtle pull at an unconscious level indicating don't establish this connection, don't join with him, because then I will be all alone.

Sam, another man in his early forties, talked about this same desire to establish more of a relationship with his father. At the same time, his mother began to remind her son that his father had been disengaged from Sam—and her—for such a long period of time that the son "better not expect much different from him." The mother stated that there was a fairly deep rift between them as a couple and that being able to reach the father probably would be an impossibility since he wasn't even relating to her at the time. She said she had tried to bridge the gap between them for years. She had tried for so long that she was about ready to give up on his father.

In fact, she had worked hard to get her husband interested. When Sam was growing up, she had suggested vacations they could take as a family, outings and camping trips for weekends. She had always taken responsibility for the three of them to be together and get closer to one another. Sam's father was very reluctant to get involved with the family, since he was in the early days of establishing a very successful real estate business. Then after Sam had left home, his mother tried to get his father to take trips with her or find similar interests, and had even asked him to be in couples therapy, which he refused.

Who can blame her for warning Sam about his father, or for being concerned that she would lose her relationship with Sam and thus be even more alone? Still, Sam had a strong need to know his father, and to give up his role as a kind of "surrogate husband" to his mother. With some coaching, Sam was able to talk with both parents about his desire to be closer to his father without cutting his mother out of his life. It has taken a good deal of work on Sam's part, understanding on his mother's side, and a kind of rude awakening on the part of Sam's father, but after all these years, there seems to be a strong hope for a healthy intimacy among these three. Sam's father had to realize that his work had become a substitute for living, and that he very nearly lost what should have been most important to him—his wife and son.

At this point, you might want to spend a few minutes looking at aspects of the dynamics in the relationships involving your mother, your father, and you. These questions will help you sort this out:

- Which parent do you feel closest to?
- Which parent seemed to have "responsibility" for your "upbringing," that is, "whose" child are you?
- Was your father strongly involved in your family activities or a kind of "peripheral" figure?
- How did your mother respond when you brought girls home: with excitement, anger, jealousy, happiness for you?
- Whom did you speak with about sex?
- Did you see your parents as a couple? Did they seem to enjoy each other? Were they clearly interested in each other? How could you tell if they were or were not?

If you found that you consistently answered in ways that indicate your mother's pervasive involvement in your life and your father's emotional detachment from you, you have evidence that a bond that might have developed with your father is missing, and you may be overly attached to your mother. We have made this statement before in this book, but it bears repeating: we are not advocating that men cut off their relationships with their mothers, distance themselves from females, or reject what positive experience they may have with women. Rather, we encourage men to use these discussions and exercises to enrich and expand their relationships to find a place for intimacy with their fathers, and with other men. In that light, we will continue to discuss the effects of "motherbinding" and absence of the father in men's lives.

What effect does being bound with the mother have on a boy as he grows up and begins to date and meet young women? This time, let's have an exercise before we begin the discussion. Please answer the following questions for yourself.

- Have you ever been without a relationship with a woman for an extended period of time? How did you feel? How self-sufficient did you feel?
- What are the physical, emotional, and intellectual qualities of women you are attracted to? How are those similar to or different from those of women you choose to spend time with, marry, or work with?
- What would your mother say about the women you are attracted to? What would she say about the women you spend time with? How do you feel about the response you might get from her in this area? Does she ever come between you and the women in your life?
- How would you compare your wife or girlfriend with your mother? What are any similarities or differences?
- What do women in your life say about your mother

and father? How would they characterize your relationship with each of your parents?

In some cases, the orbit around a mother is so strong that it excludes the potential presence of another woman in the man's life entirely. Don Hatcher was still very attached to his mother, and had very little true dating experiences, though girls found him attractive. He would meet them, and invite them over to the house, but his mother would take one look at them and curl her upper lip and that was the end of that one. The mother, at an unconscious level, perceived the other woman as such an intense threat that the power of her relationship to her son totally excluded the possibility of another woman. As a man in his mid-twenties, Don was an "unattached single," and nearly destined to become a "confirmed bachelor."

An interesting psychoanalytical study was conducted by the National Association of Medical Psychoanalysts (1956) in order to look at the origin of homosexual styles of living. Their research, biased as it may be, maintains that consistent patterns emerge not only for the "confirmed bachelor" but also for a good number of homosexual males, confirming that the intensity of the bond with the mother not only excludes the father but certainly excludes other women as well. The term for the nature of that relationship is "close binding"; it is intimate enough so that its closeness excludes strong relationships with other people. Another word for the relationship is "fusion"—the two people are fused or welded to each other and exclude others.

What happens with the young boy is that his early skewed relationships eventually become internalized patterns of how to live with others. These internalized guides then have a strong effect on future relationships. One hypothesis is that if the primary relationship is with the female, without a good, close modeling with a male, the primary internal relationship, even with a homosexual man, is heterosexual. In other words, he has a heterosexual relationship internally that is so powerful, so full, and so consuming that it does not leave room for an intimate heterosexual relationship in the external world. It leaves room only for homosexual relationships.

David, a thirty-eight-year-old homosexual, is a nonpracticing MBA. He chose business because his workaholic father advised him to do so; yet, after making the suggestion, the father lost interest in David's studies or work life. David finished his degree, found a good job in little time, but quit the job after a few months because of "personality conflicts." David had always been a "disappointment" to his ambitious father, a "fifties man" dedicated to work and sports. His mother claims she never understood David's professional dilemma, since she thinks of her son as a "wonderful, talented boy who can do anything he sets his mind to." She never liked roughhousing boys, boys who made messes or fought, as David's father had done. She preferred David's sensitive artistic personality, and found him a comfort to her.

For a good many homosexual males, their relationship with their fathers was so absent that some of their body longings are transferred to another male. In so doing, the homosexual male achieves some of the lost bonding with a male substitute and keeps the mother relationship safe, constant, and unchallenged. Of course, not all homosexual relationships are based on this model. Many homosexual men have developed deep and long-lasting relationships based on a mature and highly-developed sense of self and autonomy.

A man who is "apron-tied," however, lacks a strong internal model of closeness with a father. He grows up talking exclusively with women about what is going on inside of him, the feelings of pain he is having, and the new excitements in his life. For this man, who never has the valuable experience of intimacy with another male, there is a missing connection in identification and closeness with the same sex.

This male who "feels right" only in the sensitivity of a female relationship can look "soft" like Don Hatcher, or more like the "very masculine man" who doesn't display his feelings with other men. If you go talk to their wives, what you frequently find out is that they are very soft and clingy at home. They are very reactive, very emotional, pouting, whiney, hurt, and wounded at the slightest criticism, doubt, or questioning of any kind. They are very motherbound in the sense that they are always looking for that womb-place where they will be protected from harm. Despite the gruff exterior they show in public, these men are defending themselves against the awareness of their "apron strings." They save their woundedness for home.

Ted is a forty-two-year-old male, married with two children. He is tall and handsome, and a former college athlete. Women are drawn to him because of his good looks, quick wit, and appearance of confidence. His relationship with his wife has been volatile and erratic, with frequent episodes of verbal and physical fighting. Each accuses the other of infidelity and being unable to meet his or her needs. Ted's wife describes him at home as sullen and demanding, like a spoiled little boy who requires constant praise, support, and "buoying up." Any criticism or even hesitation to wholeheartedly agree with Ted by anyone is perceived by him as an attack, leading to angry outbursts and ultimately to Ted pouting and, at times, getting drunk.

In both the "soft" and "macho" patterns, the woman occupies a central position in the men's lives. The boy who may have received a certain amount of his nurturing and affection needs now wants to continue that special treatment in a relationship with a wife. These men spend the greater part of their dating/married life attempting to get women to adore them, need them, and be dependent upon them. Unfortunately, this attempt to find an identity in the definition by other people is doomed to failure. It is the plight of males whose style has shaped itself around a soft or macho image, that each is afraid to renounce mother's security and enduring support. Overindulgent empathy or hypervirility is used as a defense. They are running away from that which is so obvious within the confines of their own home.

Archie Bunker looks mean. He is bigoted, he is tough, and he portrays the image that no one can hurt him. But he is incredibly reactive. Everything bothers him. He is intolerant towards everything. Everything gets to him, and causes a violent reaction of some kind or another. One of his violent reactions is to the "differentness," and apparent femininity, of his son-in-law. He criticizes this and suggests that there is something fundamentally wrong with him. Yet, if you look at the times when push comes to shove, Archie falls back on Edith when he feels threatened. He could be bombastic, boasting, and bastardly; but it is always against the backdrop of having the motherly Edith supporting him, and calmly taking his yelling, rejection, and insulting of her. She is able to withstand every insult and every rejection on his part. He is able to withstand nothing. He has no tolerance. His son-in-law has tolerance, and is always suggesting to Archie greater acceptance of other people and kinder treatment of Edith.

Archie, like Don and the others described in this chapter, has problems feeling like a separate human being. Each is reactive to the presence or vulnerable to the absence of a woman in his life; each has failed to develop a solid sense of security and autonomy. How does this process of separation take place, and how does a man feel his own individuality as a person and as a man? Our next chapters describe the important role a father plays as he literally pulls the boy from mother's orbit and helps him to be reborn into the world of males.

Chapter 3

Father's Body as Challenge

The central image of the male ego is the hero. Every boy and every man harbors a fantasy of becoming a hero in one way or another. The hero combines knowledge, strength, and courage and has an impact in and on the world; he makes a mark. The roots of the word *power* suggest the meanings "ability" and "action." The hero has the capability to do something of significance, and he takes an opportunity to do so, to prove himself.

For a boy, his father is most often his first "hero" in the real world. Of course, there are teenage mutant ninja turtles—but in terms of real people, dad usually gets the vote. Father seems to have knowledge, strength, and courage. His ways, his thinking, his feelings, and especially his body are the "challenge" that the young boy encounters in his development of his sense of what a hero is.

Our word *challenge* derives from a Middle English word, *chalengen,* which has two meanings. One is "to acclaim/claim" and the other is "to accuse." A father's body is a sort of claim to territory, in that he has achieved a physical maturity and matching skills to operate in the world. Father has also staked out the territory of men, the land of the larger world which includes his occupation, reputation, avocations, his house, and a position in the family and in the community. This is his mine claim or homestake. He must assist his son to make his stake or claim in the world.

The word *accuse* comes from the Latin *accusare,* which means to bring a lawsuit. The boy challenges and accuses his father regarding the laws. The father restricts his freedom. He challenges the father's restrictions. These are the two qualities—to acclaim and to accuse.

Anyone who has been around young boys will appreciate the source of the words *acclaim* and *claim;* the Latin *clamare* means to cry out loudly, *acclamare* to exclaim or proclaim. The words have to do with noisily crying out, carrying the sense of a loud, sudden noise. Little boys often express themselves with growls, yells, various noises—onomatopoeia, like truck noises, dog noises, airplane noises. They go around proclaiming and exclaiming their presence, claiming their territory and making lots of claims for the world and against any injustice or unfairness they might see in their world.

Father represents, in this sense of challenge, the world which his son exclaims against and proclaims about and pushes against, both in the physical sense and through emotion. The father's voice is experienced as having a lot of power. His son is testing his own voice—this is part of his physical claiming and challenging. He is testing his voice against the father's voice to see if his is going to have the same power and impact on the world. Not long ago I overheard a four-year-old saying to his father, "I am the boss of you." The young boy was making his claim, his bid for power. These are some of the meanings of the word *challenge.*

Father represents a kind of vast expanse, the territory of manhood. The son lays claim to his piece of the territory, his homestake. He is claiming his own sense of manhood as he pushes up against the father and challenges the father—loudly. Little boys are great at making noise, and what parents ought to see is that it is not just "cute," it is essential for a boy to growl and make faces and mimic big machines and monsters and dinosaurs, so that he can measure and sense his growing potency. A neighbor, Linda, was having a garage sale and a friend brought over some things for her to include. One item was a toy lawnmower. It didn't make it into the sale. Tony, Linda's son, laid claim to it the minute he spied it. It was broken and had no sound. What he did was provide the sound of the lawnmower himself. He also took the lawnmower to bed with him.

Father represents an object that the boy at every age can bounce off of, and test. The father is a beacon, a rock, a pillow, all kinds of objects for the boy. He is an instrument. When a boy goes out into the world, he encounters different experiences. Some support and carry him, like floating in water. Others knock against him and will not yield to him—for example, when he falls down from his bicycle, and the concrete will not give. In the boy's earliest years, the father in his own body represents those limits of the world that later the boy finds to exist in the world itself.

Accusing Father

Generally, in late childhood and early adolescence, a son begins to see his father as being somewhat of an imposter. He posed as having been the world itself, as all-powerful (at least in the eyes of the boy), as all-knowing, and even as omnipotent. And now the son accuses: "How dare you represent that power to me, when in fact, you are not those things. You are imperfect, you are hypocritical. Instead of being all-knowing, you are pedantic, preachy." The son attempts to bring his father down by accusing him of shortcomings. Now, the son attempts to gain his father's power by using his own voice to accuse the father. The boy says, "Look, you are not the world, you are not everything. I have found that there is more of a world than you, you are not the omnipotent being you once appeared to be." This is where accusation begins.

There are accusations in which the boy, like an attorney, gathers evidence against the father for years before he actually brings his case. He watches his father's actions and accumulates his words. He looks for hypocrisies. He looks for inconsistencies in his father's statements. He watches other men to compare them favorably to his father—coaches, teachers, and the like. He accumulates data about the world and his father, and one day he indicts his father—when he is big enough and loud enough and verbal enough and brash enough.

Can you remember challenging your father?

- What was the scene? What issues were involved?
- What words or physical blows were exchanged?
- Had you imagined this happening before?
- Were things different in some ways after the challenge? How?

For fathers:

- Do you remember a significant verbal or physical challenge by your son? If so, what was it about? Did it seem to make sense to you at the time? How do you feel about it today?
- Why do you think the challenge happened at the

time(s) it did? What did you or he do to precipitate it?
- What was the outcome? Did the record get straight? How has that challenge influenced your relationship since?
- Was the incident(s) a stimulus for remembering something similar between you and your own father? What unfinished business is there between the two of you, and between your son and you? Were you finishing the business with your own father by substituting your son?

As you ask these questions, is there a big blank in memory, or an actual lack of challenge between the generations? In some families, there is such a strong prohibition against expressing feelings or opinions that nothing ever gets brought to the surface to be worked through. Some men report that their fathers were very "neutral" with them, and that anything they even attempted to bring up with their fathers just "disappeared," and was never dealt with in any significant way. If this describes your own situation, you may wish to look into the influence that the loss of the opportunity for challenging your father has had on your life. Are you looking for challenges in every area of your life in order to make up for what you missed in your family with your father? Do you overreact to any sign of power on the part of another man by immediately trying to overpower him? Or, alternatively, do you find yourself shrinking from making a challenge with other men at all? Do you collapse at the thought of challenging someone in authority? These are signs of unresolved issues with your father and insecurity in your own sense of masculinity.

Every little boy wants secretly to knock his father down and is terrified that he will be able to do so. Every grown man would like to find out if he can knock his father down and is terrified that he will not be able to do so. The little boy's terror about knocking the father down means that if he could knock his father down, the world somehow is not big enough or strong enough for him to exist in.

I saw a boy in therapy, Nate, who by the age of twelve, thought he could do anything. Literally packing his bags, he decided to go to Iraq to stop Hussein. In preadolescence, he had developed an incredible level of grandiosity. His father was a big burly sailor of a father; but whenever they wrestled, the father always let the son win, giving the boy an inflated sense of his own power. Thus the son likewise viewed the father as less powerful than he appeared. Now what had developed was an exaggerated, overrated sense of his own capabilities; he had no knowledge of his own limitations.

So it is important for the father—when the boy is very small—to let the boy push on him without collapsing. But also, to be sensitive to the boy's need to be powerful and to very clearly *pretend* to be physically impacted by the boy, and to accuse the boy loudly, "Ouch, you are hurting me! Cut that out, what are you doing? You are so strong!" but always with a smile and clear indications (such as keeping muscles loose) that this is play—not in a vicious way, but with a sense of humor to let the boy sense his power. Then in later years as the boy grows, the father adjusts to the boy's physical power, so that as he does become stronger, the irony or joking decreases concommitant with the boy's own growing power.

I remember wrestling with a kid when he was nine years old, something I do sometimes with boys who have a tendency to collapse and not want to move at all. He was a member of a preadolescent therapy group, and was complaining of multiple psychosomatic symptoms—headaches, asthma. Initially, he was a boy I had to provoke in some ways, to push and pull on him because of his past tendency to wither and whine. I had to work hard to get him to express anything at all.

I treated him for a year or so, and worked with the parents (the father was easily intimidated by women, very reactive, and prone to uncontrolled anger). The father figured out that he just didn't know how to give permission to the one boy child in the family to be strong and energetic. With my coaching, the father started encouraging his son—and also himself—to be more assertive, to use his body, and to speak up. The father and son began to work on this together. The son began to be more assertive with his voice, and to stand up taller and look people in the eye. The father began to calm down, be more reasonable, and more sensitive, and seemed more confident as well. They began to have a good influence on each other.

Some boys are very hesitant and retiring about challenging their fathers or anyone else. It can be true in these situations that the father is very tyrannical or, conversely, very shy and retiring. It can be useful for the father to do some work of his own on what "challenges" or claims he makes in his world, and the quality of these: whether they are made obnoxiously and rudely by the tyrannical father or perhaps not made at all by the shy father.

The son may need a "jump start" to get his own energy, confidence, and encouragement going. Wrestling within a therapy group, or other physical interactions where a boy (or man) can begin to exert physical strength in safe ways, has proven an effective approach for some therapists. As energy emerges, repressed feelings sometimes accompany it—anger, sadness, terror, or joy accompanying a physical excitement. When a person's feelings and body sensations are alive and moving, he can begin to initiate and move into activity, into the flow of life, with more sense of self and sense of security.

The Defeat of Father

A moment will come when the son—in some area or perhaps many areas, physically, mentally, financially, or whatever—will be able to defeat his father. So it then becomes a question of awareness of limitations and self-doubt for the father about his own power and his own ability. There is an interesting point that occurs when the father—who also had been a son, who has terror about whether he could have knocked his own father down—finds himself in a position with his son where he is not sure he can knock his own son down. Where does that leave him? Is the father now a double son, doubly challenged by the men in his family? Often, his own father's father is dead by then. Where does he find his position with the generations of men? This becomes a really difficult problem when the father fears the son could overwhelm him and the son has to decide whether to hold back his challenge to protect the fragility of his father's pride or go ahead and make his claim for power, perhaps defeating his father.

Some aspects of the story in the film *The Great Santini* are germain to this topic. First is the importance of the father and son having to deal with the inevitability of the son's increasing capacity for skill and for physicalness and the beginning of the father's decline in that area. When these two forces meet each other, what happens to the son and what happens to the father?

The father should feel some pride in seeing his son move on in a rite of passage, recognizing his son's progression as a very special moment. He may simultaneously lament that he is now in some way being surpassed by his son. The father's limits are painfully evoked. The father needs to be able to keep his own sense of power in place, yet still allow the son to exert his power, establish his own place, and make his claim.

In *The Great Santini,* the father was deeply threatened by the son's increasing claim to his own power. This culminates in a scene outside the house, where the two play basketball. After many games in the past, which the father always won, this time the son wins. The father is totally unable to recognize and accept his failure. The mother invites the son to look at his father in a different way—explaining how hard it was for the father to endure that loss, that change. Consequently, the father goes out in the rain to shoot baskets relentlessly at twelve o'clock at night. According to the mother, that should signal to the son how hard it was for him to accept this loss; and it is evidence that the son has now somehow challenged the father's number-one position as most important, strongest head of the family. The son feels nevertheless bitter—bitter that the father refuses to recognize his abilities. Thus, the son's capacity to empathize with the father is extremely small. The mother responds that maybe in time he will be able to understand what the father is feeling. In fact, he does see his father in a different light much later in the movie. He is able to see his father in a more understanding way.

One of the points we'd like to stress is that family members are often unforgiving of each other. Maybe it is important that there be a short period of bitterness on the part of the father and the son. The father's bitterness has to do with the grief he's experiencing of his own limits as a human being, as a male, and as a father. The son's bitterness concerns his accusation against the father, of representing an impossible ideal.

Idealization of a father by his son is sometimes portrayed as something pathological. We believe that this is not pathological and that it is actually healthy for a son to idealize his father and then to go through disillusionment. If he never goes through disillusionment, of course, that is when the problem arises. For the young son to idealize his father in some way, regardless of the father's behavior, is an essential step in beginning to understand the possibilities of the world of men. The father embodies a spiritual imagery that the son in his more mature years will be able to place more appropriately with God. For the moment, however, the young boy is mostly body and unconsciousness. He is mostly a body seeking form, so that early youth's idealization and later disillusionment in the father is an important process.

As a boy progresses into adolescence, he goes through a period of overpowering feeling that he can do anything. The world is his oyster. Interestingly, this attitude mirrors that of the twelve- to eighteen-month-old, who looks out at the world and imagines infinite possibilities. During the stage of adolescence, the son looks at the father, who has lost this brashness, this optimism, this sense of incredible opportunity, and accuses the father of having lost something vital. In many cases, this is indeed true of the father. He has been disillusioned about the world—something has changed, especially for the father in his late thirties or forties. He questions what he has done, what kind of mark he has made on the world. Much of what seemed important earlier in life seems less so now.

I read a quote in the newspaper that the difficult thing was not when the man woke up and realized, I am not going to be President, but the next morning when he woke up and realized, I am not going to be president of anything. For the son's development, it is as necessary to see his father as a failure as to see him as a success in his choices and accomplishments in life. It has to do with the acceptance of his father's—and his own—humanness. We are not implying that the father should collapse and break down or the son see him as a worthless person—far from it. Rather, the son should see that his father missed the mark on his highest aspirations, partly perhaps through no fault of his own, and partly through some bad choices or some limited understandings that he—the father—might have had. There is a beautiful lesson in this for both the son and the father. The son will not be ready to see it as such, but he will remember the model of moving through failure, since failure is such a valuable experience in the world and so universal. The father will have allowed the son to see him as a fallible, accessible, vulnerable person. He will gain the possibility of greater intimacy with his son. The father models the ability to remain connected even in adversity and even under fire, as his son attacks and tries to diminish him.

Frank Pittman, a noted family therapist, says that even as a young boy, he waited for his father to make some momentous fatherly pronouncements or gestures toward him. He hoped they would sit down and have these chats where the wisdom of the father would come rolling out. Or as they sat at the campfire the silence would be broken by pivotal stories of his that would take on mythic proportions. What happened instead is that they just sat in silence with the father once interjecting, "Listen to the sounds of the night." Frank hoped that his father would be, and do something, more. He went through most of his preadolescent and adolescent period looking for his father to mark him in some way and for that interchange between them to have an impact, but it never happened. He forced himself later in adult life to accept how their relationship was less than what he had hoped for or expected. And yet, in some sense, Frank was forever marked by his father—he became a potent therapist who has helped people work through their disappointments, suffering, and loss. Perhaps just being with his father and listening to the sounds of the night, and being aware of his own disappointments, helped make him a good therapist. This may have helped him listen with consciousness and empathy when he began to hear the stories of others.

I think back to my own experiences of my father and me fishing. One example that stands out is a parallel in some way to Pittman's story. When I would go stay at my parents' cabin, I would like to get up really early and go fishing. I have rarely met anyone who gets up as full of energy to go fishing as I do. My father is not exactly obsessed about fishing in the way that I am—he likes it, but not to the same degree. Anyway, I would get up very early to go down to the boat at the dock and he would get up too. I could tell that he really did not want to be up that early in the morning. Having worked a seventy-hour week, he looked bad. He looked tired. His color was spectral. Before he could even get going to the dock to go fishing, he had to get a big thermos of coffee into himself first. But what I remember so clearly about him on those mornings was that he never complained about getting up to go with me. He would come down to the dock, obviously feeling awful, but he was always cheerful about coming down to go fishing with me. He would give me a slanted grin and say, "Good morning, young man! Ready to go fishing?" He was in a good humor. There was something more critical than his own physical discomfort and the way that he might do things. There was something more important in going along with me. Naturally there were a number of times he could be highly controlling, grouchy or bitchy, and nasty. But this was one of the situations in which he joined with me in my excitement about something I genuinely enjoyed and cared about. I am sure that after having gotten up at five o'clock in the morning six days of the week, he sure as hell didn't want to get up another morning at four-thirty. Still, he chose to do that. There was something really nice about him just plain doing it without making any kind of a big deal about it. Often today, when I don't feel like doing something, or get tired of other people around me, I remember my father's willingness to walk down to the dock to go fishing with me at five in the morning.

I remember the last time I was asked to join my father's adult male golf group, because one of the players cancelled. My score was better than anyone else's in the group, but most especially it was better than my father's. He had some reputation for skill. I remember that the next day, when we were working side by side, I brought it up in a brash way: "That was a pretty good game yesterday, huh? I'm sure you probably noticed that I beat you." He expressed annoyance at my bringing the subject up. He said there was really no need for me to say that. I somehow began to believe that was the reason I was never included again.

So my own personal experience, at least at one level, is that by surpassing my dad and by my even mentioning it, I alienated him. I threatened him when he was not ready to accept that as a reality. I was the usurper. Interestingly enough, two years ago, my father, my brother, and I played together in a tournament. Our team won. We played against teams of my father's peers, older doctors, and the like, that he had worked with for a generation. He was proud of me winning the low score of everyone in the entire tournament. Also, he exuded pride about going up and accepting the winning trophy. I just couldn't help but reflect about how things had come full circle.

As I look back over that time, there seemed to be a period of some bitterness on his part that was probably important for him to stew on for a while and then to get over. I was also bitter and frustrated by the lack of recognition and the belief that there was something wrong about my staking my claim on that territory. Whatever tension was between us seems more settled now; time and maturing has helped us both.

My father's education was only through high school. Still, he managed to do very well in the corporate world. Toward the end of his career, he had engineers, lawyers, and Ph.D.'s working for him. Everyone working for him had more of an education than he did. For as long as I can recall until the last few years he bitterly complained about "educated jackasses." I think he was threatened and had a lot of inferiorities about his intellect, but defended himself by running these guys down. I took it personally for many years, since I got advanced degrees and wasn't making much money, but I finally realized it was his own inner security he was defending, and that I was pretty upset with myself for not being more of a success in the business world like him. Recently, he has just started asking me questions about things I am interested in. Having just retired a couple of years ago, he seems to realize—as I do also—how much time we lost staying in this "stand-off." He wants to know how my career is going and what I am doing with my time.

He came to see my office, and asked questions about my practice.

I think I made my academic choices in part to challenge him, to stake out my own territory, and once I was set on being an intellectual and he was set on being an anti-intellectual, the battle lines were drawn. So there has been a long period of bitterness between us, which now seems to be ending. I am asking him more and more about his own life, about his excitements and interests and experiences, and he is doing the same with me. Also, he had some resentments toward my work in art, since I have had some success in that area as well. Now, since he has retired, he has started doing wood carving, and has given me two beautiful animals he carved, which seem very symbolic of the carving out of our relationship that is taking place at this time. This gives us more to talk about since we share a common interest in craft. We are now sharing interest in each other's lives. He has finally seemed to let go and is accepting of my achievements in my area and I of his in his own. We no longer feel as bitter or strained when we are together. This is a big change.

The son's challenge to the father is an important developmental milestone for both. As the son makes his claim to manhood, he loses some of the precious illusions of youth, yet gains solidity, maturity, and resiliency. The father, at first charmed by his boy's adoration, must ultimately survive his later accusations of falsehood and hypocrisy. Even as he accepts some of these attacks as truths about himself (and thus builds substance from this ownership), the father recaptures part of his own adolescent fervor for truth and unlimited opportunity by being made aware of these issues in himself. Father and son, son and father—each gives birth to the other's claim to his place in the order of men.

Chapter 4

Father's Body as Shield

Imagine a toddler, just starting to get up and walk. He is unsteady. This world outside of the womb is interesting, but full of things to run into—gravity which works against him, angry dogs (his own size or even bigger), and stairs to fall down. Some of the time, he would just rather go back to "being a baby," to being taken care of, held, and rocked. He would just as soon give up that sense of himself and be taken care of by mom.

What the presence of the father does is to help the son avert being lost in the maternal orbit. The father buffers and protects the son from being swallowed up by the force of togetherness and undifferentiation, that pole of dependency, that movement toward union. The boy feels a pull to the womb, where there is security without risk, and without disappointment. He feels a strong desire to stay an infant and be suckled by mother forever. The father, in some ways, forbids the son to get stuck in such a state, but rather gives him a push, his first move toward being an individual.

A father and mother work together to help the boy move toward his own sense of independence and achievement, though the father represents to the toddler the one human being closely connected with the mother who is a separate being from her. He thus models individuation. I am reminded of a mother and father who were toilet training their first child, a son of two and a half years. At the end of the first frustrating day of training, the boy sat in his little potty and said in a dejected tone, "Mommy, this is too hard, just put me back in diapers!" Through mom and dad's empathy with his frustration and their gentle support, he was able in a relatively short time to achieve the goal of independent use of the toilet. His parents knew how close they came to giving in to the temptation of letting their son slip backward to infancy rather than forward to becoming a young boy developing his own sense of individuation. They were particularly aware of the importance of the father's loving but steady insistence in helping the boy in this, and in later tough moments in his development.

A boy uses his father's acceptance and support as well as his hardness and his courage to block and to thwart the insults and the hardships of the world. The son uses the father to help him cushion and absorb some of the disappointments and frustrations that he encounters. The first important separation and loss has to do with his relationship with his mother and later on with a multitude of losses and hardships. It is almost as if the father helps shelter the son from some of the darkness and some of the rain and the cold until he is ready to go out into the light.

There are two, seemingly contradictory, impacts of the father as shield, both of which are necessary. Our word *shield* comes from an Indo-European base which means "to cut, cleave, or split" and also from a Lithuanian word meaning "to slice." Normally we view the shield as a kind of protection against cutting or splitting, especially by the sword. So there is, on the one hand, the sense of the father cushioning or protecting the son from the world and from physical harm and from undue pain; and at the same time, behind the shield, he is pushing the son and encouraging the son to split away from the domestic world, the world of the mother. And eventually, behind the shield—here I think of the Greek word for shield, *aegis*—under the aegis of growth and development, father gradually pushes the son to forge his own shield against the world, and to split away from him—the father—as well.

The shield is a protection against the world and a way to enter the world by protecting oneself. The shield has both active and reactive dimensions. The reactive part is the one that buffers and protects and shields; but there is an active dimension where there is the "cleaving"—becoming your own separate person and developing your own shield, protection, and boundaries, as you enter the world.

When a knight goes into battle, his shield is what protects him from the attacks of others. It is also what allows him to move into the battle. It acts as the most forward running part of the body, the part that enters the battle first. The shield becomes a kind of boundary, a powerful edge of the body which helps the young person enter the world and enter the battle—the world of competition, prowess, and turmoil.

A father can begin actively to teach his son how to approach conflict when the boy is a toddler. Entering conflict without a shield, without the ability to protect oneself—either through denying that there is conflict or collapsing—is self-annihilating and purposeless. A shield serves the purpose of creating an edge, a boundary for the body, both to prevent self-destruction or destruction by others. The boundaries provide a way of "pushing in" to conflict, but not "rushing in." A father can teach his son that conflict is not a bad thing, that it is a natural part of life, and that the son need not fear it or shy away from it.

When a baby is born, he completely identifies with the mother and, in some part of him, would like to remain forever in that world without risk and without disappointment. As he begins to experience himself as a separate person, in the early months and later into life, he needs to learn how to actively enter that world of conflict. The father can provide a sense of this boundary through his own body. The boy will stand by him or behind him when he is angry at his mother, or afraid of her. The father can encourage him to express his feelings in an appropriate way. He can help him express this anger or fear without trying to overwhelm his mother or be overwhelmed in the process.

Imagine a father (or mother) teaching a son to ride a bicycle. He starts by stabilizing the bicycle and walking along holding it steady. He helps the son experience a sense of balance and a sense of being able to hold himself upright even when forces might be pushing against him, such as gravity or a bouncy sidewalk. Father holds on long enough until he feels that his son has acquired a sense of his own balance. This provides the son with an immediate body awareness that he can keep his balance. At a certain point the father gives a little push and lets go so the boy can ride on his own. The father expects that the boy will be hurt or fall off at some point. Still, the son now has a sense that balance is something that can be maintained even when conflict arises, and even when the bumps and slick places are encountered.

Let us extend the earlier metaphor of the knight. The knight's shield carried a certain insignia. Sometimes the insignia was an animal which symbolized a particular virtue or strength. Often it was an emblem of a value that the knight held dear. With every knight there was an apprentice or "shield bearer." The apprentice learned about being a knight by the two spending time together. Later on, from what he learned, he might move on and develop his own feel for knighthood, having had a basis under the tutelage of the knight.

When the son has a shield, he is able to define his own boundaries, his dignity, and sense of value and morality. This is the part of the shield that the son takes with him, and then he makes his own mark in the world. But how many sons carry their father's shield, or their own, with pride and dignity?

What the knight does with his apprentice, the father does with his son—the father or the knight allows the apprentice or son to merge with his own strength, his own calm, his own caring, his own serenity, and his own confidence. The son or shield bearer feels a certain kind of nobility or goodness as he merges with something bigger than himself. He uses that sense as a way to build something secure, that sense of balance. Later, when he moves out into the world and adds distinction or his own uniqueness to the insignia of the shield, he perhaps adds further qualities of confidence and potency to the mark of fatherhood.

One of the gifts from the father is a vision of the world which includes an appropriate sense of the balance of danger and safety. If the son is not taught about both of those possibilities, he is unprepared to enter the world. He has to know that there are dangers of possible attack and what those dangers are. He needs to know about counterattack and the virtues and techniques of deflecting attack. The shield that the father provides in terms of danger has to do with teaching how to use the shield to one's best advantage in counterattacking. The son learns how to move the aggressor or opponent into a corner or into a place where the opponent is more vulnerable.

We might think of the father teaching the son appropriate models of self-defense, whether these be physical or otherwise. He can perhaps teach the son how to "fight back," using his body. Or he can teach his son the skills of verbal or psychological self-defense when attacked, how to counterattack and use knowledge, words, and images to defend his own ground from attack. It is certainly true that one day an attack will come. Though the father might imagine a more innocent world for his son, if he forgets to teach the son self-defense, he is laying the boy open for abuse. Persecutors easily sniff out victims.

There are other times when it is more important to know how to deflect attacks, by simply "sending them somewhere else." The sense of a shield in this case has to do with understanding the difference between an attack made against oneself and the attack really meant for someone else.

Charlie, a successful architect, was devastated at one point in his career by the physical collapse of a building project with which he was associated. Although he was not in any way responsible for the accident, his reputation was damaged. He conducted himself during this time with integrity and forceful action, however, regardless of the embarrassment and fear for his future that he felt inside, refusing to hide or hang his head with shame. His adolescent son, aware of the stress this situation put on his father, was able to gain a measure of respect for his father's courage. He expressed this respect aloud to his father, who was deeply touched by his son's appreciation of him. The exchange between them was one of deep intimacy and appreciation for each other.

What are some methods of deflection a father can teach a son? He can teach him how to "absorb a blow," like a boxer. The father of a friend of ours taught him that if a man attacks you, you should respond, "I will take your criticism and consider it for twenty-four hours. If I find it is true, I will return to thank you for pointing it out to me. If it is not true, you will not hear from me again, because I will know that you have incorrectly insulted me." This is a method for absorbing and deflecting attack which takes into account one's own limits and one's own narrow self-perception in the moment. It is a defense which is not "defensive." If I use this method, I do not allow myself to be devastated, either. The goal is to learn to accept criticism that is due and appropriate and to reject criticism which is simply an attack, and to take the time necessary to consider the difference. Perhaps one of the primary gifts of the shield is to help along that sense of discerning what is appropriate judgment leveled by other people.

One essential gift fathers can give their sons is the model of being able to absorb hurt, disappointment, and sorrow and be able to "stand it," and go on. We are not referring to a macho image of stoically withstanding pain or denying that pain has any impact. Rather, it is important for the father to pass on the self-knowledge and trust that one will not fall apart, shatter, or disappear under confrontation or disappointment. We are talking about faith in oneself, proving that one can "tolerate" whatever comes along. A father can teach and model the appropriate absorption of criticism with the adolescent son. A perfect time is when the son "accuses" the father, in his "bringing his father to trial," as we discussed earlier.

Perhaps the father's most important job during his son's late adolescence is to hear the "accusations" of the son and not be devastated, to accept what is right in the criticisms or accusations and to reject or fairly defend himself against those which are wrong. The key is for the father to remain in the relationship at this time, to continue to stay with his son regardless of the injustice or justice of the son's accusations of the father's hypocrisies, limitations, or failures. This "remaining involved" demonstrates the power of the shield to the son in a way that words, descriptions, admonitions, or suggestions cannot accomplish.

For the younger boy—who may imagine that his father is a monster or a demon or that he himself carries a monster inside of him—the key thing is for the father to simply remain with the son, to stay there, through the boy's fits of anger and tantrums, and not overreact or punish the boy for normal emotion. The father also must direct the boy to contain the emotion—within time limits, within limits of safety to property, house, and bodies. He must also teach him to differentiate between expression of feeling and vengefulness, that is, to air his emotions and opinions without being abusive toward others. Additionally, the son must be exposed to ideas and values that do not coincide with those of his father, and see his father exposed to these ideas, and then see that his father can tolerate difference from himself, that he weathers confrontation and challenge. These are types of shielding and containing that allow an understanding for boy and father alike of the simultaneous experience of danger and safety.

Chico and his wife, Laura, currently have custody of Emilio, his fifteen-year-old nephew. Emilio's mother and father died a year ago in an automobile accident. At times, Emilio will blow up with rage when asked to do chores or when Chico says no to his demands for money or to be taken places across town on a whim. Chico has worked hard at not being reactive with Emilio when he gets rageful and stomps around the house, and has tried to help the boy work through his sense of injustice, sadness, and deep anger at losing his parents. Chico hangs in there with Emilio even when the boy is nasty, obnoxious, and rude. He also has taught his nephew to use a punching bag to drain off angry energy in his body. He is trying his best to "be there" for a boy who is going through a very painful and confused period of his life.

There are so many men in the world today that have not experienced this essential sense of "containment" and recognition. These men were not permitted to be in proximity of the father and experience significant emotion without the father being overwhelmed or defensive. Many of these sons were significantly criticized, humiliated, or embarrassed for their strong feelings. What they carry with them is a fear of being hurt, both physically and emotionally.

Two types of men can develop from deficiencies in containment and recognition. One type denies his potential for being hurt. He fights constantly, runs headlong into hurt, and shows no fear of being hurt. What we know is that this man denies the frightening aspects of the situations he ceaselessly thrusts himself into. On the other side are men who carry this sense of being physically hurt by other men and women. They tend to defend themselves against the possibility of being hurt. They avoid conflict at all costs, staying clear of any tough situations. They just don't feel secure in standing up to adversity. They believe they will be hurt (physically or emotionally) badly and feel threatened all of the time. They don't know if they'll be able to tolerate life. There is an open-woundedness about them that leaves them without a kind of basic skin or solidity for life. They cannot discern well between wrongful attack and good, purposeful criticism. They don't know what they will be able to withstand, but believe that they won't survive any form of conflict.

In the first case, the tough guys—the men who are constantly fighting and seeking conflict—are always entering the world with a sword, but no shield. They have to keep the sword in constant movement. They don't make careful, discrete cuts into the world, but wild, slashing motions to keep their own bodies safe. So the sword always has to be moving, to keep others at a distance. Their protection is really offensive; they carry no shield. They have never learned the sense of shield, or the appropriate use of the sword.

In the second case, these men are hiding behind the shield; they really have no sword. Their weapon is invisibility. The shield they carry may not be marked by the father. In fact, it is really not a masculine shield. It is the placenta—the feminine shield. They are hiding at the edges of the womb, rather than behind a separate and moveable shield with which they can take charge and enter the world. There is a kind of shrinking away into infancy whenever conflict is encountered. In fact, this last group of men doesn't even get into conflict. They have an uncanny, a really telepathic, ability to spot conflict a long, long way off and hide or make themselves invisible long before the conflict actually occurs.

Stephen, age twenty-nine, came to therapy because of depression and anxiety. He described himself as "panicky" any time conflict arose in his job. Whenever another man would raise his voice, disagree with Stephen about something, or confront him on something he thought was being done wrong, Stephen would shake inside, feeling like a little boy who could not defend himself. He firmly believed he could not think for himself nor protect himself. In the course of therapy he learned that he did have the ability to set boundaries with other people, that he did not have to sit back and wince every time conflict came his way. He began to practice projecting his voice, loudly, and to state his opinions or ideas with this voice. In a few months, he found himself able to stand up for himself very well at work. He began to know something of the "judicious use of the sword."

On the one end of this spectrum are the tough guys. They enter the world on the attack or the offensive, never allowing closeness with other people to develop. They continuously sever any links or bonds. Their sense of shield is splitting or cutting. A man who uses himself in this way sees the world as an opponent. He is always prepared for ambush. He believes that the best defense is first strike. The only safety is in getting in the first punch.

The second vision also still sees the world as dangerous, but feels that the best protection is hiding and retreating from the world. He returns to the warm, undifferentiated world of mother's uterus, where conflicts are taken care of by mother. Men who conduct their lives in this way also do not allow closeness to develop with other people, since they disappear from conflict, which is an essential ingredient of relationships. These men *seem* to be more involved in relationships. They will talk about being close and actually get warm and cuddly, but the other person must become a uterus, a haven of warmth, of quietness and slow heartbeats.

A mature, masculine approach is practiced by a man or a woman who enters the world with both the sword and the shield, knowing the need for self-defense and possessing the capacity to enter conflict with the sword available. Also, masculine is a good discernment of the most effective moments to disappear or become invisible to the opponent.

Early in the book we defined masculine as synonymous with strength, determination, straightforwardness, virility, courage, tenacity, and firmness. These qualities of the masculine require both the ability to fight and the ability not to fight, to remain calm. An effective warrior is one who is not afraid of conflict, but respects it, and who has a broad range of weapons and shields available to him. Sometimes one needs to enter a situation with the sword cutting and moving; sometimes the sword can merely be showing with one's hand nearby. Sometimes the shield is best used as a kind of distraction; the insignia, that reflection of character, tells a great deal to the opponent.

Think concretely about the father, in a practical sense, teaching his son about concepts of the shield and the sword. The image that may come to mind is a father who directly or indirectly teaches his son how to use his body to wrestle or box. This teaches the son how to shield, how to protect, how to move offensively, how to move defensively, what it is like to be hurt, and what it is like to hurt. This is done in a safe environment, where the intent of the interaction is learning and experimentation.

There are situations in which men can teach boys the specific skills of self-defense—boxing, wrestling, judo, karate. At the same time, while doing these things, they must be taught key values. The father or other teacher must say, "I am going to teach you something in order for you to protect yourself. That does not mean that with this skill, you should go out and pick fights in order to do something to someone you know doesn't know how to fight." The master in the *Karate Kid* movies taught his young apprentice skill as well as the values of constraint, containment, pride, and justice.

Also, specific instruction on the part of the father with

regard to many dangers in the world is necessary. This can take many forms. For example, fathers should actively attend to and discuss music, movies, television, drug use, driving the car, hitchhiking, or dangerous sports with their sons. No kid likes this, but it is the father's responsibility to discuss the values and dangers—and importance and good points as he sees them—of what the son likes and the activities he engages in. In this regard, it is also his responsibility to try his best to see value in what his son shows interest in, and not simply dismiss it if it happens to be unfamiliar to him.

Many men today at the age of fatherhood grew up in a time when they believed that children—especially adolescent children—should be able to choose whatever they wanted in life. They view this freedom to choose as a very high value. Therefore, these fathers are very hesitant to "impose values" on their children. There is a difference between imposition of values and a steadfast commitment to particular values. If a father requires his son to believe or view things a particular way, and he will not hear of any other possibility, that is imposition. If he does not make a responsible attempt to understand his son's point of view, or an honest attempt to consider what might be wrong with his own beliefs, or if he simply tries to "lay down the law" with his children, that is tyranny.

But the steadfast commitment to a set of values is a different kind of thing, a necessary thing in a father. This means that the father holds particular viewpoints and will do a certain amount of censoring with the child about what he will allow in his house, in terms of literature, videos, music, and the like. The father will have to decide for himself what his own positions and values are in relation to the things he will censor. He will be able to state a viable reason for censoring material, something much beyond the simple, "because I said so." He will demonstrate an openness to discussion and dialogue, to the viewpoints of other people, though he may be strongly committed to his own values.

This is a very difficult process. If a father becomes rigid or unmoving, he has missed the point entirely. If he becomes passive and permissive, he is also wide of the mark. It means that the father has to become actively engaged in knowing himself as well. It means looking into his values and into beliefs and perhaps discovering things about himself that are surprising, shocking, or extraordinary. He may find an aspect of himself more strict, more puritanical, more conservative than his own father, whom he saw as very rigid and uptight. On the other hand, he may find that the things he assumed he rejected or frowned upon are really not so bad, and that he would support himself and his son looking into or doing them. He might find different or even opposing thoughts and feelings on such topics as sexual preference, music, spiritual experience, or money.

The father's commitment to himself is, of course, as important as his commitment to his son. These two commitments are interrelated in such a way as to be inseparable. One important thing, then, a concrete thing that fathers can do, is to become acquainted with what young people are interested in, to really know the music, movies, and literature young people are intrigued by before judging them out of hand. He may take a "descent into hell" and allow himself to listen (by himself) to his son's music or watch a video recommended by the son, informing the son that "just because I am taking a look at this doesn't mean I am condoning it! I just want to know what it is you are getting into so I have a better sense of what you are about."

The father has to consider his own values, not just receive them from the pulpit and then push "playback" and spill them onto his son. This won't work, never has worked, and never will. The problem here is that kids have what Hemingway called a "foolproof bullshit detector," and they know immediately if father is spouting received values or playing it straight with them and has thought over what he is regurgitating.

It is valuable for fathers to know about the dilemmas that boys are facing today. It won't kill fathers to talk, to have a dialogue, or to be aware of what situations are creating conflict for their sons. It is naive to ask children to "just say no to drugs," for example. It is absurd to make one statement and expect it to make any impact on the son.

For the son to use the shield properly, he will have to know something of the cost and the consequences, and the impact of saying "yes." What does "no" mean? Does this mean being ostracized from a group at school, perhaps from the brightest, most creative, most interesting, most active kids in the school? (Listen up . . . it is not only the "goofballs," the sleezy and social outcasts who are using drugs. Fathers, wake up!)

Fathers—many of them—need to take a good look at their own drug use. If they expect respect from their boys—let us hope fathers still want respect from their boys—they might well turn on their own, perhaps rusty, "bullshit detectors" and look at what ways they are delinquent and "just saying yes" to drugs and alcohol.

The role of the father is clear. As he invites and occasionally pushes his son into the world, he must arm him with the ability to take care of himself. The challenge of the father is to teach his son how to actively defend himself, decipher safety from danger, and to act aggressively, when needed, to protect himself. The task of the father is to shield his son from the harshness of the world until he is ready to absorb it. And while the son is under that protection, he will need to grow into his own strength, and develop his own capability to discern what is right. A father who makes the commitment to guide his son into the world gives his son an invaluable gift of potency, and in the process, takes his place with all the fathers from current and previous lifetimes who have done their duty.

Chapter 5

Father's Body as Womb

In certain traditional societies, such as among the Australian aborigines, there was a complex group of rituals which created the image and experience of the father as a male mother. One of the most important rituals was the creation of a male womb. The male womb, even though it was a representation of the female womb, was an important symbol for the young man because it represented a birth into the male world.

A small hut or small arch of sticks and leaves were built. The father would climb on top of this pile. The boy of around twelve years was placed inside the opening. After much screaming and hollering, the boy was pulled out of the opening. In some versions of the ceremony, the celebrants even cut the father so he would bleed and the blood would fall on the son.

The boy was drawn out of the "womb" by other adult males in the tribe, to be born a second time, this time of the male mother and the male womb. This time he would be initiated into the secret mysteries of the male world.

The boy was then separated from the mother's—the

women's—world. He was taken away from the mother, dragged away from her. She and the other women would be screaming and crying ritualistically (and probably sincerely as well) in grief over the loss of her son. This created a symbolic death for the boy. His childhood was over. Now he was to be reborn, as a man.

This image, though very dramatic and more exaggerated than what we might see enacted today, symbolizes in a graphic way the process of growth into manhood of young boys of all cultures. The boy moves from a life in the world of his mother toward discovering his own sex and a world apart from the mother, the world of men.

The symbolic value of this kind of ritual is something we have very little concept of in our current culture. We have some facsimiles of this, examples of boys being welcomed into all-male groups. But for the most part they tend to be oriented to the same age-group, rather than with a range of ages directed by the elders. They do have the quality of ritual and of bonding as males. Fraternities, all-male clubs (which are disappearing at a high rate), and sports teams all perform rituals in effect.

Rookies in the camps of professional football teams, for example, are required to sing their alma mater in the mess hall as well as any other songs that the veterans may request. This is one example of a ritual for inviting the young man into a different world—the world of professional football as opposed to the protected world of college football and college life. This is performed by a wide range of individuals at several ages, led by the "elders" of the team.

You can find isolated, good examples of these kinds of symbolic initiation events which carry on some of the same tradition, such as those in sports teams, fraternities, scouting, and the like. But, by contrast, in most traditional societies we have records of, every boy had to go through a clearly defined set of rituals that would help him make the transition into manhood. Perhaps one of the greatest losses for the modern or contemporary boy is the sense of the collective support.

Possibly the best remaining example today is the bar mitzvah. In this tradition, a boy, at his thirteenth birthday becomes personally responsible for all of his actions and he accepts all of the laws of his religion upon himself. Through this ceremony, he is lifted into the world not only of the rabbi and his father, but of the adult world in general. He can demonstrate in a very clearly prescribed way and in a very democratic way, that he has made the transition into the world of the grown-ups and the world of men. The Jewish tradition has recognized and maintained the importance of male—and female—initiation.

One loss for many boys in today's world is the lack of concrete participation of older males in their process of growing up. Christians have lost the tradition of the spiritual director. In elementary and secondary education, we do not have an active mentor system in the schools, but rather we lump people together in groups with an emphasis on quantitative learning. Some schools do have a system in which teachers are assigned a certain number of "advisees" and have the opportunity to get to know these individual students—and the students to get to know an individual teacher—on a more individual basis. One problem, of course, is that teachers are already overworked, and schools understaffed, so a concrete solution is difficult to come by. Nonetheless, with our "mass production" system of education, there is very little attention to what some think is the most effective (albeit idealized) form of learning—a good teacher on one end of a log and an interested student on the other.

Some opportunities for working with a mentor exist in

graduate schools, and informally in undergraduate schools. Many professions, as well, have mentor systems, such as publishing, design, and law. Two disadvantages to these forms of initiation, however, are: (1) only those who go on to professional fields get these opportunities, thus leaving out the majority of the population; and (2) these initiations come rather late in the development of men and women, rather than at key times, such as the onset of puberty and during the burgeoning of intellectual curiosity in the teen years.

If a boy is not involved in sports or an all-male organization of some kind, there are very few places where he can find this collective initiation. Even within sports and the bar mitzvah tradition, the direct collective participation of older males in the boy's life is lacking throughout the adolescent years. Boys are set adrift and somehow are supposed—one day—to have been transformed into men. How can this happen without direct instruction and guidance? We don't ask people to learn algebra without instruction, and algebra is much simpler to learn than manhood.

The initiations which are available seem to involve a limited number of boys. A number of the organizations that do offer "ritual" ceremonies, participation, and membership offer rituals that are demeaning, embarrassing, humiliating, and do not carry with them the actual rite of passage and birth into the world of men. What is needed is a kind of "welcoming," against the backdrop of a sustaining and supportive group, that will make joining something of value and worth which makes this difficult "rebirth" worthwhile.

This is much different from the traditional practice of hazing. This is less an activity of welcoming young men into the world of older males than a form of self-serving and abusive ridicule of younger boys by older boys.

A father can actively engage and help his son enter the world of men and manhood. One meaningful way to fulfill this would be to gather the generations of men. A father, if his father, his uncles, and his brothers are still alive, can gather these generations together at certain key points to officially create a ceremony for his son at certain ages. This would be of particular importance at early and late adolescence—key times to gather to honor the boy in some way, to recognize his growth, development, and potential.

This could serve as exciting and healing revelation for all of the men involved, not only for the boy. It would offer a sense of continuity, family, and regeneration of manhood and maleness, a kind of healing in its vivid, visceral immediacy—an experience that can be felt in the gut. The generations gathered makes a strong image. This much male energy pulsing through the blood of generations would make a powerful moment. It would provide a time for welcoming the boy into the world of men, but also a moment for the elders to kindle their inner child, in other words, revive the internal, youthful, dreaming, and aspiring young man in their own psyche. This is one way that an exciting ritual could be created among families. It might take some doing, because of how families have spread through the country. But it might be a very good reason to draw the men together for something other than a funeral or a wedding—something that indicates the continuity of the men as something parallel to and as important as the "civil" events in life. It is an honoring of maleness, something that we could go a long way in recovering here.

Specific celebrations of momentous occasions could be recognized as well. A simple example might be when a boy gets his driver's license. In this act, the boy obtains the permission and energy to move freely and powerfully in the community. He gets permission from his society and the law to transport himself and others throughout the community—really, anywhere! Think of it. We are saying to this boy of sixteen, we trust you with this extremely fast, powerful, potentially very dangerous thing—a car. After all, a car can be dangerous, uncontrollable, even abused, and able to cause serious injury or death. What kind of impression is made when several generations of men in a family take a ride with the new driver? Rituals of this kind can have a tremendous impact on people, and can make a big difference to the driver. They give him both a symbolic and a concrete awareness of the responsibility that such a transition means.

Another issue regards the use of alcohol. It is absurd to think that boys under eighteen are not going to drink alcohol in our culture. All of our literature and all of our social awareness around drinking has to do with personal responsibility. Yet, it is a delusion to ask a boy to accept the entirety of social responsibility at this time without the guidance of older men; he cannot, therefore, he will not. This is the father's—and other men's—responsibility. They must be directly involved with the young man, because it is a collective responsibility to him. When a young man is moving freely in the society and is given permission to intoxicate himself by the community, it is also a collective responsibility for the father and other males to take this possibility seriously. To ignore this responsibility is to shirk their duty to themselves and to the boys, because the young men will drink, are drinking, and few of us are paying attention to this.

So it is important for the older men to participate in some way. Each father will have to decide how to do this in his own fashion. One guide to consider is to use alcohol only on those occasions when it is part of a ritual or ceremony, for example, a toast at a rehearsal dinner the day before a wedding, the wine at Passover Seder, or a graduation celebration. The amount of alcohol will be very limited because the intent is to celebrate and honor the occasion, and not to get high or lose control. It is against the law to serve alcohol to minors, and we don't recommend it without considerable reservation. Each father has to make up his own mind on how to deal with this difficult question. However, what will not do is simply to ignore the issue. The key is to emphasize the ceremonial quality. If you want kids to take drinking and drugs seriously, you have to take them seriously. Between a father and a son, the father can create a very powerful impact by taking a drink with the son—with awareness that the drink is a powerful agent.

When drinking or drugs are taken within a peer group or just within a certain age group, there is not the power of the community. There is no mature male to measure the behavior. When kids drink together, they think nothing of it. It is an "ordinary" experience. They "party" together. They have little awareness that they have invited Death to the party. They do not comprehend the full responsibility of drinking. Parties of teenagers should never be without at least one-third of the assembled guests being adults, and alcohol and drugs should not be allowed at all. This is not necessarily to "police" the kids—though the Greek word *polis* means "the collective, the community." It is to *polis* the kids, to remind them and never allow them to forget that if they are participating in the dangers of adulthood, they require the presence of adults who care about their community and will not allow the reckless and careless destruction of it.

How did it happen that men grew afraid of boys, so that they no longer *polis* them? We see boys running freely in the streets with no adult male supervision, bent on activities which lead to self-destruction. The fathers today cannot control them because they have not been initiated into the world of men. There were no rebirth huts for them, and they have never entered the "men's hut" themselves. They know little about what it is to be a grown-up man.

When the father is involved in a boy's development, this solidifies and embodies an experience as real for a boy. The father's love, containment, and limits, make a boy understand that there is meaning and value in the world. A father's participation earmarks conditions which require respect and thought, by marking events between father and son and bridging the generations. Life is brought to a new level, a level of interconnectedness and responsibility between the generations and between men as a group, giving self-awareness of masculinity and its meaning.

By the father and son participating in something seemingly mundane, a ceremonial or collective meaning develops. A ritualistic quality might emerge as a father and son take a cross-country trek together. Father and son alternatively driving to a particular location might seal a special bond. Their destination might be a place which holds a special mystique for them or something of common interest—canoeing, hunting, golfing, or hiking. It could be a music festival, a museum, a monument, or a site where something historical happened within their own family.

When Luke turned sixteen, he and his father launched their raft in the swift Colorado River rapids. It was just the two of them, for six days, camping, cooking, and paddling. Luke had known this trip was coming for several years, since his father had also taken similar trips with his two older brothers when they turned sixteen. The raft trip was a rite of passage for each son, an initiation by their father into the world of men. Luke's father had also taken a trip on this river when he was a boy; he had always remembered that trip, full of danger, excitement, the majesty of nature, and late nights with coyotes all around and his father in a sleeping bag next to him under the bright night sky in the mountains.

Meccas exist everywhere. Everywhere is the center of the world when we recognize it as such. When a father and son go somewhere together, even in their own neighborhood, they should strive for a certain awareness of their contributing to the continuity of the generations together. This seemingly mundane event serves to tie the bond between men. Of course, it is a bit much for a father and son to consciously believe that every time they go out for pizza it is a "holy event"—it isn't. However, this deep bond between them is developing on an unconscious level at all times, whether they are aware of it or not.

Another enriching bond between father and son could be forged by the father treating the son as an apprentice. The father can instruct the son in something he knows about intimately. This can be something the father does with his hands, some information that he has learned, something that carries a place in his heart, his mind, and his body. Every man holds within him the keys to knowledge of his particular passion.

Of primary importance is the father taking time to instruct the son in this particular area that is meaningful to him. The significant thing is not only the passing on of information or skill, though this certainly holds real value. Most critical is the opening to the son of the father's heart, the demonstration and sharing of his passions with the son—that is the real meaning of this apprenticeship. Even the son, who may feel minor interest in the topic, learns a great deal. He sees his father's passions, his vulnerability, and his energies. The son can see how his father moves, how he breathes, how he thinks and feels in these moments, and at close range. The energy exchange in such moments can be very powerful, and can form images and body experiences which the son may feel for many years.

Conversely, the son, if he has a particular area of passion, should be allowed to instruct the father as well. I noted a fine example of this exchange between father and son in my own neighborhood. The father has a strong fascination for the American Civil War, which is evident in his collection of mementos, videotapes, and artifacts. The son, in contrast, is obsessed with baseball and with baseball cards. The son is now sixteen. Just recently they decided on two Sundays to spend time in each other's chosen area of interest. Last Saturday, the two embarked on a trip to Arkansas, to the Pea Ridge Battleground. There they would survey a celebrated Civil War battleground. This Sunday, they are going to a baseball card show at a trade mart here in town. Their agreed-upon program sets up a ritual, a symbolic exchange which invites both the father and the son into a masculine world together.

For this purpose, I have carried on a tradition in my family. I am the only one of the three boys in my family who carried on my father's interest in raising vegetables and tending a garden. This is a real passion with me, as it has been for my father over many years. If I search I can't really identify a logical reason to continue this practice (it is not true that you can raise vegetables cheaper than you can buy them in the store; it actually costs a lot more to raise them). I think it has to do with continuing my connection with my father in some way. Interestingly, both of my children have already shown a keen interest in planting and cultivating.

This is a yearly ritual that occurs in terms of cleaning up the garden and getting it ready for planting and seeding by hand. Perhaps each child will ask for a little piece of ground for his or her own, in time.

It does not matter what the interests are that are shared. Our hope is that fathers will invite their sons into the world of manhood in whatever ways they can find, and that they will take this as a sacred task, with powerful responsibility.

Warren has found a consuming interest in the genealogy of his family, especially on his father's side. He has spent time reading family records, visiting old gravesites and parcels of land where homesteads once stood. As he is finding the seeds of his family's history, he also invited his fourteen-year-old son to be a part of that journey. Though Garrett doesn't share all his father's enthusiasm, he has spent many hours with his father scouring the countryside at old sites for remnants of the family's past. Garrett is witness to his dad's passion as well as his wish to show his son the history of his forefathers. Garrett has carried out this genealogy search in his own studies by using the exciting history of a distant relative (a gold miner in California) for a social studies project and speech, a project which was very successful, received with interest by his teacher and his fellow students as well. Garrett's success in the project has added to his enthusiasm in accompanying his father in this family odyssey.

- What do you remember about participation in ritual-like activities with your father? Are there any you can recall? If so, what was the meaning of this for you? Did this involve shared interests?
- What rituals would you like to develop in your present life, with relatives, friends, your son, or with other people you know?

- Are you involved in any activities which include groups of fathers and sons? How about groups that have older men as participants? Where might you go to get to know some older men?
- Do you know what your son or other young men and boys are up to today? Have you talked over their interests with any of them, with a son or with other young males? If not, why not? If yes, what is the outcome of these discussions?

Fathers should see their sons as reflections of them. We are not saying that the sons will naturally or simply follow the father's highest values in the near or distant future. What we are suggesting is that fathers have shirked their responsibility to see that their sons are strongly influenced by them.

The son ought not to be a servant or a mirror of the father, however. The son has to be able to choose whether his father's ways of thinking and behaving are what he wants or not. Father and son need to take a hard look at what they believe. This tough questioning of themselves takes on a special importance when sons are choosing religious or political perspectives, professions they want to follow, and moral or ethical commitments they will stand for.

Fathers who have "worked their way up" the socioeconomic ladder from poverty to financial success, who have suffered on account of deeply held values such as religious preference, or who have loyally followed deeply ingrained intergenerational patterns of ways of life may have an especially hard time when sons do not make choices exactly as they have. They may hope their sons share the same passions and commitments they do. They may be somewhat blind to the fact that their sons are only vaguely interested, or minimally talented, in the areas they themselves have developed to forge a path in life. They may wish for their sons to carry forward unfulfilled dreams of their own, and they may be in for some big disappointments.

Some fathers may think it right to step out of the son's decision making under the mistaken idea that they are doing their sons a favor by "not interfering." Their approach may be well intentioned, but it is not ultimately useful to either son or father. These fathers squander the opportunity to share their passions, dreams, and hopes with their sons for their lives as well as for their own. Thus, father and son never know each other well, the son never gets the valuable chance to "challenge" his father, and the son lacks the useful image of the father's image of what he may be or do in life. Even sons who choose very differently from their fathers profit from whatever positive or well-meaning images their fathers have of what their sons' futures might be. They have a home base to respond to, either to choose or to choose against.

The antidote to either of these excesses, too much or too little involvement, is for father and son to ask of themselves and of each other whether each is following what he really thinks is right, valuable, and a "good fit" for him. The following questions might help in this process.

For the father:

- How did you go about choosing and defining your morals, values, job choice, personal interests?
- Who was most instrumental in your making these choices?
- Have you discussed your values and interests with your father? If not, why?
- How would you feel if your son showed little interest or respect for what you hold as important in life? If you would be angry or disappointed, how do you

account for this?

- How would you feel if he was passionately interested in the same things as you? Would you be happy, or think that he was trying to "take over" something of yours? How do you account for the feelings you have?
- As your son is (was) growing up, do you notice that you have particular hopes and ambitions for his participation in certain events (sports, music, outdoor activities, reading) and do you hope that he would come to particular decisions similar to or different than yours?
- Do (did) you find yourself living vicariously through your son's achievements in various areas? Do you grieve the loss of your own youth when you see him doing certain things?

For the son:

- How has your father introduced his values or interests to you: forcefully, as an option, as an unquestioned expectation of your acceptance, or as a dialogue with him taking the lead?
- Does your father (in your view) seem overidentified, or alternatively, uninterested in your values, achievements, or failures?
- Are you aware of having made choices in life with the hope of pleasing your father; or, on the other hand, of attempting to provoke a response from him?
- Do your values, interests, and moral choices feel right to you, in your own heart, or are they the ones you hope your father would approve of—or reject strongly?

If the answers to the above questions seem consistently to indicate that father seeks unquestioning compliance from his son, or that the son rejects and attempts to provoke his father outright, this indicates a failure by father and son to reach each other, a failure to achieve a meaningful dialogue. If either extreme—strong compliance or scornful rejection—is indicated, then you have work to do.

Fathers who find that they demand compliance can change their approach by seeing their sons as people who may need their guidance, but ultimately will make their own choices. They can begin to offer themselves, their time and energies, rather than trying to impose themselves and their views on their sons. They may grieve their own lost dreams, pain that might have occurred by their being expected to comply, or effort spent to achieve that has resulted in hardship and weariness.

Fathers who find themselves distant and detached from their sons can realize that their ideas, feelings, and emotional contact is important to their sons, and that their model and guidance are essential stepping stones to their sons' development.

Adult sons who have found themselves overcomplying or bitterly reacting to their fathers and what their fathers "stand for" should work on their own autonomy. This does not mean throwing away their fathers. Rather, it means finding out what they believe, what they would choose outside of their fathers' (or others') influence, what they think and feel. These values and feelings can be worked on successfully by many men in discussion with friends, in support groups, or in therapy.

Instruction for a father on how to raise a son cannot be given or followed like a recipe. You have to do more than choose events or spend time together, though this is a good start. It is not enough, either, to be simply educational, to teach a son how to do something, though that too has its place. Many men get stuck in wanting to dictate what is right and not making themselves vulnerable, available, or responsible; yet, these are the keys to the process.

The father's active involvement does make a kind of "womb" for his son. There is something inherently nourishing in the relationship of a loving father and his son. In the mother's womb there is a give and take between the body of the mother and that of the son, a rhythmic exchange. Food and oxygen move from mother to fetus. Toxins are screened out for the defenseless baby, which keeps him nourished and safe.

Similarly, a father can take responsibility with his son to help monitor toxins. It is his duty to monitor and screen harmful or poisonous material that comes in his son's way, in terms of movies, music, friends, literature, and drugs. It is essential for the father to be involved very actively in screening material for a boy under twelve years of age, very stringently when the boy is small, and with some decrease as he gets older. He will not be 100 percent effective, of course, nor should he expect himself to be, since a son will have to live in a culture where dangers exist and he will have to learn to respond to them.

Adolescent-age sons will require and accept less direct scrutiny of what they encounter, but a father still has the responsibility to know what is occurring in his son's world, to know about his school system, his teachers, friends, activities, projects, pastimes. A lazy, hands-off approach is irresponsible and even possibly criminal. One father in our men's group discovered that his son had been stealing electronics equipment on a regular basis from stores and cars, and storing these things in his room; he had approximately

$24,000 worth of stolen merchandise in there. The son had also been making long-distance phone calls to a "phone sex" outfit, and had ordered fifty-three X-rated videotapes on his father's Visa card. The father only discovered his son's activities when he noticed a huge phone bill, couldn't figure out what the calls were about, and called the number to find out what it was. He had quite a shock. This was a well-meaning father who simply hadn't taken the time or effort to be interested in his son's life.

We are reintroducing the idea of censorship for children. This is a healthy idea, when practiced with sensitivity. It is the father's (and mother's) fundamental responsibility to sensitively censor what his children encounter, to introduce his son to new ideas and information, and to make sure his son knows as much about the world as possible at a rate which is reasonable and takes into consideration the child's age. The father should actively state and work for what he believes in, and make certain that these beliefs promote compassion, understanding, self-awareness, and self-responsibility.

This approach means some censoring of a boy's television, music, and reading material. The son will gripe and argue about the censorship, and that is fertile ground for dialogue about values and beliefs. Practiced judiciously—by this we mean with good will and thoughtfulness—censorship promotes the son finding his own values, since he sees his father modeling good judgment. When censorship is practiced maliciously, to simply eliminate what the father is unfamiliar with or afraid of, it has the effect of alienating children and other people.

A womb contains and envelops. Parents should help their children cope with the onslaught of overwhelming and contradictory demands. One man we know has a son whose basketball skills have already prompted scholarship offers from ten major colleges. This father has worked hard with his son to help him make the choice of what school he will attend. He has helped him find information, has discussed with him at length the pros and cons of each decision. The father has given his own opinion and openly admitted that he has a particular bias, and what his bias is. And now he has left his son to make up his own mind; the son knows that his father is proud of him and will respect his decision, whatever it might be.

The story of a basketball star may seem like a set of glamorous options, each of which is positive, and none of which would be bad. What about some tough cases, ones in which kids with rough street lives have to choose each day whether or not to sell drugs? The cases are similar, however. Many kids, lured by the prospect of large incomes or other amenities—the prospect of wanton consumerism—will be tempted to be victims of promoters who in some cases are simply street hoods with better offices. Cases are rampant in professional sports, particularly in the example of boxing.

If we lived in ancient times in a village on the edge of a forest, we wouldn't let our children go into the forest or outside the village parameters without proper adult supervision, because they might be eaten by animals, or captured by another tribe. No parent would let a child wander off like this. Yet our children are in jeopardy with some of the information or images they get from our culture. Children are exposed to pictures of deviant or casual sexuality, drug usage, and the wanton destruction of property by characters in shows or rock stars on MTV who seem to think such things are funny. Themes of self-destruction, despair and rejection of parents or school flood the ears and eyes of young children and young adults as they watch rock videos.

What are kids supposed to believe? A boy who watches television for hours each day, without regular discussion and modeling of a good father, is ripe for entering a life of addiction, disrespect for other people, and shallow, meaningless relationships with other people and with his own inner life.

Are today's media images less dangerous than yesterday's threat of wild animals in the forest? The dangers may seem more subtle than a Bengal tiger. But this is because we have grown numb to images of violence, abuse, and addiction through our constant contact with them. They have become familiar to us, and hardly affect us anymore. A person getting shot with a machine gun on television has no more effect on today's teenager than perhaps a little jolt of excitement.

We know now from studies of the last hundred years that images often have the same or greater impact than direct bodily experience. Images can directly affect emotional, physical, and spiritual health just as much as bodily impact. For example we know that in sexual abuse cases, though a child might not have been actually touched, a child who was treated emotionally as a sexual object can demonstrate the same pathology as one who was physically abused. The child's bodily response, psychological response, and view of self and others can be just as severely impaired by such treatment.

So what happens when a boy watches a movie in which a child is pornographically used? The child watching that experience is raped. To see a child—or an adult—unprotected or used pornographically or hurt without protection can have the same impact as the direct abuse of the child. So to ask a father to actively censor his young children's material is simply to ask that he (and the mother as well) perform one of the essential acts of parenthood—protection of children.

Even adolescents who buck at any restraint of what they choose to read or watch are not immune to confusing messages. Behind the bravado and false confidence lie children who are struggling to find a solid self-identity and who change in their emotional states constantly; one day they are acting very adult-like and the next day (or hour), like a two-year-old. This is an essential time for the active participation of the father in his son's life. The need for protection, though lessened or changed somewhat in the case of the adolescent, is still necessary for the internal security of the child.

We repeat, as a caution to fathers, that censorship can be abused. The child can be overprotected by parents who abuse their power. Again, we stress that a father's example and discussion of his beliefs are a mighty influence on a child or adolescent. Young men will experiment and find out about life, and sometimes do very dangerous things on their own. This can't be ruled out. Sons need to learn of values and beliefs that their fathers have, and of values and beliefs different from those of their parents. If their parents have exemplified desirable beliefs and have been emotionally close to their children, the adolescent should be able to encounter dissenting viewpoints without being brainwashed.

The necessity for the father to be actively and honestly involved in the son's building of his value system cannot be overestimated. This is an extraordinarily important element in the boy's development. Father—and mother—provide a kind of womb, a base from which the boy moves into the world to make his choices, develop, and grow into responsible adulthood and citizenship.

Chapter 6

Managing Pain and Grief

Addictions

Mark Hunter is a good-looking man in his early thirties, tall, lean, and still in pretty good shape. He exercises regularly and has done so since the "glory days" of his high school football career when he was a tight end and a very successful pass receiver. He is doing well financially, and sells medical equipment for one of the larger companies in the field. He was, in fact, among the top five in regional sales last year. Well liked by his customers and colleagues alike, he is considered a "hell of a guy." He has a pricey apartment in the city, beautifully furnished, a BMW, and a sailboat.

Mark was one of the most popular boys in high school. He has always had a girlfriend—or several at the same time. Two years ago, he met Evelyn—"Evie," a professional woman—at the church he attends regularly, and began the longest relationship he has ever had. The two of them were married last year, and Mark was certain that Evie was the woman for him and that things would really work out well this time.

Problems began right after the wedding, when the two of them started living together. Mark accused Evie of "wanting me to be perfect," of demanding too much of him, and of trying to keep him "dwelling" on her all the time. Evie told Mark on many occasions that he was "just not available." She told him that she was "tired of his distance," of his flare-ups followed by sullen hours of "the silent treatment." His obsession with diet was a source of irritation, his dissatisfaction with "everything about everybody," and his constant restlessness disturbed her. And his continued "using" of her things without asking—her music tapes, her computer, her car—upset her. Even while they were dating, Mark's behavior was wanting. He'd arrive at her apartment for dinner, and would immediately say upon entering, "I've got to use the phone." More often than not he would be calling a store about the price of some electronic toy he had just heard about, or checking with a friend who had "just gotten into town." When Evie would complain about his talking when the dinner was growing cold, he'd say "Damn it, Evie, Lou just got to town and I haven't seen him for years!"

Mark had numerous friends—better said, good acquaintances. When asked who his best friend was, or his two or three best friends—a couple of men he might be able to speak with very openly—Mark drew a blank and then said defensively, "I could tell anything to any of the guys I know. They are great guys!"

Evie had struck a particular vulnerability with one of her last comments to Mark before they decided to separate. She called Mark an "addict." Mark was furious at her for this comment. His uncle had died of cirrhosis of the liver from his alcoholism, and Mark had "sworn" never to be an alcoholic like him. He had "occasionally" used street drugs—amphetamines during a couple of tough "pressure" periods at work, barbiturates "for the jitters"—and admitted that he had drunk to unconsciousness "a few times," but adamantly did not consider himself an "addict," certainly when compared to a lot of men he knew!

It didn't take much investigation on my part to discover what Evie was talking about when she used the term "addict," however, and to ascertain that her use of the word was quite correct. Mark was indeed rarely using the kinds of street drugs we usually think of when we use the term addict. But he was using a large quantity of substances which are quite readily available in any large grocery story. He was smoking two packs of cigarettes a day; drinking fifteen cups of coffee and three or four diet drinks with caffeine a day; using caffeine pills and sleeping pills; regularly using over-the-counter cold medicines (even sometimes when he had no cold), alternating between the "may cause drowsiness" type and the "no drowsiness" type to get sedation and stimulation; using hunger suppressants (stimulants); eating large amounts of various foods—highly salted, heavily proteinated, or sugar saturated; taking diahrrea medicines of various types; and using aspirins and other pain relievers.

In addition to consumption of drugs, many of Mark's "habits" showed clearly defined patterns of "addiction." When Mark awoke in the morning, he would immediately call two different telephone weather reports; then he would call a general number to see how his mutual funds were doing. He pressed Evie, ordinarily a slow waker in the morning, to have sex with him nearly every morning. While eating his breakfast, he held the remote control for the television in his hand and "zipped" the channels from station to station, looking at any one program for only a matter of seconds. He called his bank account number to check his balance. Then he looked through the sports scores from the night before, swearing if his favorite teams lost and exclaiming if they won.

As she was moving out, Evie told Mark that he ought to get some therapy. She admitted that she had started seeing a therapist herself. Mark asked her if she would come back to him if he would. She made no promises but gave him an answer ambiguous enough that he, in his desperation, could easily fill in with his fantasies. She said, "I can't say I wouldn't come back. I definitely would like to see you get some help."

When Evie described Mark as an addict, she used two words that graphically represented aspects of him: "restless" and "dissatisfied." Like so many men today, Mark was painfully restless, desperate, and dissatisfied when he came to my office—and painfully angry and confused about his life. Nothing made sense to him. He couldn't explain why he was so edgy, so uncomfortable all the time. He had a good job, was doing what he liked in his spare time, and was well liked. Why couldn't he settle down, feel relaxed? Why couldn't he "keep" a relationship with a woman?

As Mark sat down in the chair opposite me, I could sense the visceral anxiety in this man, his pain and discomfort. Like most men, he believed that coming to therapy is a "sign of weakness." His only "excuse" for coming for therapy was to find a way to "get Evie back" and then get out of therapy; he was "doing this for her." Squirming in his chair, wild-eyed and looking very much like a caged tiger, Mark made his initial comment, by now a comment extremely familiar to me in my work with men: "I am very skeptical of this therapy stuff, I just want you to know that."

"I respect that skepticism, and encourage you to question everything I do or say," I answered. My respect of this viewpoint is genuine. After all, why should Mark—or any man brought up in our culture—trust the process of working on a relationship with others or with his inner life? He had no models of men doing any such thing. I might as well be his tour guide to Saturn, or ask him to walk blindfolded into the Grand Canyon, as far as he was concerned. "Furthermore," I continued, "I want you to know that this is an evaluation session—a two-way evaluation session—for each of us to decide whether we can work with each other. You have the freedom to decide whether to work with me and I with you. Therapy with me might not be right for you. Therapy itself might not be what you want. But I see that you are here for an initial session anyway, so let's see what comes out of a couple of hours together. Fair enough?" Visibly relieved, Mark settled a bit in his chair, smiled a little and said, "OK, but I am skeptical, just so you know that." "I've got it," I laughed. Mark's skepticism had already become more of a "challenge" rather than an outright rejection and his slight softening pointed to a tiny beginning of awareness and difference in Mark's life.

What I found out about Mark during that two-hour session and the next few sessions was a picture whose rough outlines are far too familiar to me in my work with men, and in my own personal experiences. Mark was a man who felt very "unattached," very disconnected, cut off from other people, from his family, from nature, from his own feelings and even—ironic for an athlete, yet common—from his own body. Mark's various addictions—to drugs, alcohol, work, sex, food, activity, information, images, Evie's attention—were attempts to escape his desperateness to escape his restlessness, his frenzied attempts to "fix" what was "wrong." And Mark is not unusual among American men. Most American men feel this kind of restlessness, and many attempt to "fix" it with addictions. Addictions are an attempt to soothe bodies that are untouched and hearts that are not warmed. Addictions are a sign of "unattachment." Addictions signal a lack of bonding with other people, with the physical world, with the body.

When a man (or woman) is not tied or attached to other people, to the place he lives, or to his own body, he experiences a sense of emptiness and hopelessness. He tries to meet a very deep, essential need through the use of artificial regulators in order to soothe a pervasive sense of despair.

- What is the substance or activity you are mostly likely to abuse?
  - alcohol
  - cocaine
  - marijuana
  - pain medications
  - food
  - exercise
  - gambling
  - sex
  - TV
  - work
  - other (name)
- What kinds of stress and anxiety occur which stimulate your use or abuse?
- What effect do you get from its use?
- Does your use seem to solve the immediate tension or stress?
- Does your addiction or obsession tend to run in your family?
- What are the consequences that have occurred because of your abuse pattern?
  - financial
  - employment

physical health
legal difficulties
relationship problems
other (specify)

- Have you tried to do without your addictions? What has worked? If nothing has worked, what has kept you from being successful?

Addiction in any form, whether it be through the use of drugs, alcohol, excessive eating, shopping, or sex demonstrates a dissatisfaction with the body's normal regulating processes. The body is experienced as too slow, too fast, having too much or too little, and an addict turns to artificial regulators, chemicals or shifts in excitement levels to try to "correct" the body. Mark Hunter's compulsive use of drugs and other substances is a tragic example of this mistrust and fear men have of their bodies.

The addict is seeking a kind of bettered or "perfect" experience, with the idea that by adding something to the normal rhythms of the body, or by changing or "correcting" through a "potion" or activity, he can find an experience of wholeness or perfect regulation. Sometimes this might be a regulation toward a sense of peace or quiet and other times toward high excitation. But the addicted person always has a basic lack of trust in the body, a lack of trust in the body's own ability to regulate itself, to cope with sensations, feelings, fantasies, and thoughts. There is a lack of trust in the body and a belief that one must use something external to make up for the imperfections in speed, in sensation, and in the way the body is reacting to the world.

External regulators are also used in order to modify some kind of disturbing sensation, such as anxiety, tension, or depression. Outside regulators can also be used as an excitation stimulator if there is a quality of deadness in the body—to kick it up, to charge it, or to "whip it into shape."

There is a sense of missing something—of an inadequacy in the body. Drugs, sex, shopping, food—all are used to stimulate a sense of "rightness" or continuity that the person believes he cannot internally produce. He does not trust that the body will react or know how to adjust. Furthermore, there is usually a history of dissatisfaction in what the body will do, left to its own resources.

Addicted men (and women) who do not have a basic trust in their bodies will not wait for the normal cycles of the body to occur. It is not that they cannot wait, but that they refuse to wait. They don't have a model of trusting, waiting, believing, or living through an experience. You can see this behavior even outside of the realm of addiction. When someone contracts a minor illness, like a cold, we know that sometimes the greatest wisdom has been to go to bed, drink plenty of liquids, and get rest. The body will naturally develop its own resistance, and combat the virus, and process it out. It readjusts itself back into wellness.

What most people do is take antihistamines and charge right on into work, as if nothing were happening in the body. This behavior may imply an impatience, a mistrust, even a hatred directed at the body. An attempt to force the body to correct itself faster and through artificial means has a backlash. The symptom will simply shift into another part of the body. It will in all probability cause greater damage of one kind or another. There are side-effects to even the most seemingly harmless drugs, such as aspirin or caffeine. This is body hatred, a revenge on the body for not providing exactly the demanded response, as if we were nothing more than machines.

Addictions generally serve as a replacement for personal energy. As we discussed in previous chapters about the relationship between father and son (and mother and son), the sense of personal energy and personal power first develop in the earliest years of a person's life. We discussed the internal sense of an ability to manage oneself and to interact with the world in powerful and meaningful ways. This seems to be lacking in the addict—that sense of personal energy, that sense of personal potency.

There is a desperate need to replace the absence of personal energy with something external, be it the over-intake of food—normally used in proper amounts to create natural energy—drugs, or other substitutes. This indicates a basic distrust of the body. In Mark Hunter's life, we see this lack of solid self-identity which he tries to make up for by surrounding himself with toys. He tries to pump himself up with drugs and to distract himself from paying attention to his pain.

Trust in the body emanates from trust in one's connection with other people—especially father and mother. That bond invites a connectedness with other people and a connectedness with self—a trust in natural processes.

Underlying a great deal of addictive behavior is a basic impatience, and a lack of bonding with other people. Part of the impatience comes from impatient parenting. Parents frequently are in a hurry, charging out into life, not taking time to be with their children (fathers, and now even mothers as well). They show little patience with their children. Young children need to be able to experience moving at their own rate—which is often quite slow—to develop, learn, and grow. Children as individuals need to learn to feel empowered, at the pace that fits their own character, in their own way.

Mark's parents were always in a hurry for him to "grow up and be a man." By the time Mark was twelve, his father got him started investing his lawn-mowing money in mutual funds and poring over the stock reports. Mark worked from the age of thirteen, and spent most of his summer days at jobs, trying to "gather a nest egg" for future wealth. Whenever Mark would question one of his parents' statements or ideas, they would say, "Well, we will help you pack your bags any day you are ready to move out and pay your own rent and groceries." So although they encouraged him to grow up, they discouraged him from finding his own way of doing things, a bind that many young people feel caught in today.

Hurry and an impatience are easily communicated to children. The children then become impatient with themselves, not trusting that if they wait a little longer, or if they take some time with something, their body and mind will be able to find a way to achieve, feel powerful, and feel all right. We ask kids to grow up fast. Nine- and ten-year-old boys out playing football are being eyed as college or professional athletes. Young kids are being quickly led to believe that they have to have certain possessions in order to be okay, to be normal.

A twelve-year-old in my neighborhood is thinking about how quickly she can get a Mercedes Benz. She wants one now, but she knows she will have to wait "a couple years," but expects to own one by then. There is an inevitable trap there for her. She intuitively "knows" that her own rate of development and her own experience as a twelve-year-old is "inadequate" somehow. She feels compelled not only to enter into the adult world but to enter the adult world at the highest economic level and at the quickest pace, owning the most, the biggest, and the best. The desire to *have,* the wish, even the felt need to own expensive objects is really alarmingly widespread among today's kids.

Giving up addictions and recovering your natural vitality is a difficult process. It requires attention to your habits, thoughts, and feelings. It can be frightening to discover what you have been doing to yourself through addictions, and strenuous to make the decision to live without them—and then to follow through on this decision. Recovery from addictions requires first recognizing what your addictions are (awareness), a decision to give them up, and then gathering the resources, guidance, and support to help you accomplish your recovery.

As part of this process, we offer the following visualization* as a step in discovering within yourself the awareness of addictions and internal resources for change and recovery. This guided imagery can work well in a group or can be done by two people.

Begin by finding a quiet place to lie down or sit, and to release all the tension in your body. Find a place where you can stretch out and will not be bothered. Let the chair or floor support you. Take several deep breaths. As you inhale, imagine that you are inhaling peaceful, calm energy. As you exhale, let out tension and breathe into areas of tightness. With each exhalation, allow yourself to carry the oxygen more and more deeply into your body. Imagine that it is going into every cell of your body. Again, as you exhale, imagine that you are sending away nervousness, tightness, difficulties that you have experienced.

Pay attention to each part of your body to see that you are resting and letting go of tension throughout your body. Tense each place that feels tight even more for a moment, and let it relax. Feel supported by the surface you are resting on.

*Contributed by Joel Vogt, a counselor and art therapist.

Now, begin by imagining that you are lying outdoors, in a place that appeals to you, where you have not been before. Imagine that it is a bright but softly lighted day. The weather is mild. Imagine that you are at peace with yourself as you begin this journey. Imagine that you can feel the breeze moving over you; experience the smells and colors that are around you.

Look in each direction and see what the landscape holds. Trees? Grass? Are there signs of wildlife? Now, as you slowly begin to look in the distance, you will see a path. It is on this path that you must walk.

When you are ready, stand up in your imagination and begin your journey. Begin walking on your path. You will notice that the path goes downward. Notice the path. Be aware of the characteristics of the path, whether it is rocky or smooth, curving or straight, narrow or wide.

Soon you will come to a dark woods, into which the path continues to slope downwards. Continue on the path farther and farther down until you reach a cave opening which is under a cliff.

There is a ledge and some steep steps which you must descend to get to the cave. Be aware that this journey involves looking for all the things you will have to face in looking at your addictions. As you climb over the ledge, be aware of the feelings you are experiencing as you approach the cave's entrance. This process will take all the strength you have to summon as well as all the tools you have learned to bring with you. Climb down off the ledge. Before you reach the bottom of the stairs and enter the cave, take a light, a torch, or any other equipment which you have provided for this journey. Standing at the entrance to the cave, be aware of the things which you have brought, and how they will sustain you. If you are not ready for this step, do not go any further. Stop and return.

If you choose to continue, you will see all the difficulty of this path and the sacrifices and risks you must take. Using the torch, you begin the long journey into this dark place. As you move away from the light of day and enter the cave, be aware of the feelings that you have. These will be similar to the feelings you will feel as you give up your addictions. These feelings can be felt, can be experienced. You can stand it and you will be able to reach the other side. Many have traveled this path before. You are not alone in this experience.

As you move through the cave, be aware that you are not only discovering pain and self-doubt. You will also discover the solidness of the rocks, and the damp smell of the rocks that carry with them a sense of the deep solidity of life. Be aware of both the negative and the positive aspects of this journey.

Surprisingly, as you are moving along, you begin to see a light. As you begin to move toward this light, you will be able to feel more clarity in yourself, and less of a sense of oppressive darkness. Moving further on, you will come to a space where you can see more and more light. As you move into this lighted space, you will be aware of more and more details of the place surrounding you.

This is a clear and peaceful place which you have come to. In this place you will feel safe and hopeful. In this place you will have peace of mind. This is a place you can come to any time you choose. It is yours. It is your safe place. It is a place you have found to return to when you face the darkness of your addictions.

Congratulate yourself! You can stay here for as long as you wish. Take your time to look around, to soak up this place, to make it solidly a part of your awareness. Look in each direction, left, right, up, down, in front of you, and behind you. Each direction has something specific and special to offer you. As you look in each direction, be aware of what different qualities can be yours from what you notice in each direction. Take the time to notice each of these features.

Then, when you are finished and have decided that you are ready to return, come back to your starting place. This time, without going through the cave, you will discover a new path, a new way to return. This new path of return to the beginning place can be used to return again and again. This is a new path you have created for yourself in the light of your safe place. It is one which you have found and made for yourself.

As you return, bring with you all the awareness, images, thoughts, and feelings you have experienced during this journey.

After this exercise, there are some things you can do to consolidate your new awareness. Here we suggest questions to ask yourself, suggestions for further work, and ways of affirming the work you have done.

1. What tools did you take with you? What do they offer you? How are they reflections of the strengths you now possess?
2. What are both the negative and positive aspects of your journey? Make lists of each.
3. Draw each of the directions in the "place of light," the safe place you found. What does each direction have to offer you?
4. Write in a journal what you experienced at each stage of the journey. Write what you learned, what you saw about yourself.
5. What was it like to go through the cave? What did you see there? What are the addictions that you discovered there? What did you find that you didn't

know about? Were there any surprises?
6. Write any goals that you have for yourself which will take you in the direction of giving up addictions.
7. What do you know will give you faith when you "can't stand it," and feel some hopelessness? What has come of this journey that can be helpful to you in these moments?

How can kids remain as children, staying with their own cycles and their own rhythms? It is difficult, since they are expected to grow up so quickly, as we have discovered in our clinical practices. Many have to resort to external, artificial stimulation to "keep up," and thus at an early age they begin to use drugs, sex, and alcohol, so they can "hurry and grow up." They have been taught that it's not OK to be a child. As you might expect, they lose their childhood in the process.

We are all born with a built-in furnace and storehouse of energy. As we grow, so does our ability to push, to drive and experience our own natural energy. When children are shifted out of this natural development at its own pace, they lose contact with this basic source of energy. As they continue to grow and become physically more powerful, they gradually learn to ignore their inner, natural rhythms. This explains the popularity of recent literature which invites us to "contact the inner child" within us and reconnect with our own body, our own energy, our own motivations.

Sometimes children need the slow cycling and developing of energy that comes naturally with the body's processes rather than to be hurried to the demands of a "driven" world. Unfortunately, our society is a model of drivenness. And some people even describe an experience beyond that of drivenness, which they call "riddenness." These people are actually being ridden by their addictions, like a horse riding its master, being in control.

Many children and adults feel that they are being ridden by external forces, schedules, productivity, and dollars. Children pick up the ways of their environment very quickly. The obvious example for adolescents today is on MTV. When they turn on MTV what they see in video after video is inordinately rich rock stars, living a life driven by the desire for extraordinary fortunes. This is in stark contrast to the idealizing of the sixties rock stars, who embodied a bohemian existence and espoused a simpler lifestyle (many were drugged out, however). We see images of rock stars before audiences of a hundred thousand people screaming in ecstasy in adoration of the star. They drive the most luxurious automobiles, drink champagne, zip off in their own personal jets, don extreme makeup, wear ornate jewelry, demolish beautiful pieces of art at a whim, live in palatial mansions, use expensive drugs, and consume goods at an outstanding rate.

The model young boys are growing up with is that these rock stars epitomize the highest values: of being driven and wanting to consume vigorously. The body is not to be regulated through its own natural processes, but through external sources. In the meantime, the boys passively watch videos, viewing images of "potency" in consumption, using, and acquiring.

In contrast, I remember as a young boy walking in the fields down by the creek near our house. A slow rhythm pervaded the day, as the sun moved higher overhead, the rabbits ran in the cornfield. The creek moved by at its own lazy rate. I would fish, fall into a short sleep. Then I would get up and hunt squirrels. Later, the sun would get low on the horizon and the colors in the sky would change. I had a sense that there was no hurry and there was a natural time that nothing could change. The day was going to progress at its own rate no matter what I did or what anybody did. The animals had their own rhythms of coming out early in the morning, resting in the middle of the day, foraging in the evening. The birds were awake at a certain time, beginning to move. A deer might come through the woods and then rest in an opening in the field. The fish were going to bite at their own rate, when they were ready—not when I wanted them to, because I always wanted them to, but only when they were ready.

Some sense of that natural rhythm in the world is really lacking in most of our boys today, even those in the small towns. Even the smallest towns now have cable or satellite television reception. You can go to small towns and see the same graffiti you might see in Los Angeles inscribed all over the place. Extraordinary!

For a boy, the earliest model for the rhythms of the male body is his father or other men. The father serves as a kind of model for bodily energy regulation in the world. The interaction that a young boy has with his father, that and the model of their relationship, is the model of the regulation of energy that the boy will carry into the world. So if the father is impatient, hurried, driven, or ridden, addicted in one way or another to work or to alcohol or to acquiring goods, the son very likely also will manifest this form of regulating his own personal power or energy, unless he has other very powerful models, either in his mother, other adults, or perhaps in an older sibling.

The father does model to the son how to deal with daily life, how to regulate stress, how to regulate closeness and distance, and the importance of achievement and productivity. In fact, there are many fathers who pass on to their sons a model of coldness, an inability to bond or unattachment, as well as the use of illusory substitutes for happiness. The young boy latches on to illusions that gratification, satisfaction, the sense of comfort with self can be acquired, bought, achieved through will power, or gotten forcefully through "control." Natural needs for being close, for being affirmed, for being touched are lost and abandoned. These illusions are based on the fantasy of the values of monetary achievement, success, prestige, and wealth. They are often described as the ultimate goals to define potency. Unfortunately, too many fathers become aware too late that the illusion is false, merely an empty shell. When achievement fails to deliver the desired satisfaction and confidence, fear and panic set in, followed by a form of disillusionment and hopelessness. The achievement illusion seems so inviting and alluring; however, it fails sooner or later for all men who are devoted to it.

Rather than deal with their own disillusionment, many men invite their sons to accept the illusions of achievement and acquisition. They want their sons to take over and to act that out for them, to live out their unlived fantasies, so that they can hope again. We see fathers molding sons for the family business, pushing for high grades and Ivy League schools, and vicariously living through their son's sports accomplishments. Fathers hand over to their sons an empty fantasy, and a model of chasing addictions.

Men often begin to give up and become hopeless because of their own impatience with the rhythms of experience and the slow, often uncontrollable pace of their bodies. Why? Men are afraid of being lost and abandoned, as they rush to "keep up" with the world around them. They fear that falling behind, "walking" instead of "running," will destroy them entirely. Addiction becomes a way to guard the illusion of keeping up and controlling the world. Mark Hunter's life was structured in such a way as to give him the illusion that with all his information and monitoring of his assets, he could control his fear of being lost and overwhelmed. In the end, his wife left him and he could only comfort himself with his gadgets and bank accounts.

For many men, the addiction itself becomes the carrier of the possibilities. So, for example, if I begin to use cocaine and find that with the use of cocaine, I feel infused with energy and go out and make sales, I get the sense that I can achieve again. I begin to think I can make something happen "with a little help from my friend." However, what I have just done is make cocaine the salesman. The illusion might be that cocaine is only helping me make the sale. But I know somewhere that the cocaine is making the sale happen and it is not really me at all. At some level, every addict knows that there is a difference between him and his addiction, that they are different beings.

There is a book by Lewis Hyde called Alcohol and Poetry: John Berryman and the Booze Talking. Hyde distinguishes between the poetry of the great poet John Berryman and the poetry of the Booze. He says that at a certain point in Berryman's career, when Berryman moved far into his alcoholism, the booze took over and Berryman lost his own voice. The Booze spoke in its own voice, in poetry of self-pity and self aggrandizement, the poetry of wallowing in negative emotions—the various signs described by AA as "stinkin' thinkin.'"

The individual who becomes an addict becomes passive in relation to the body. The "other" takes over. We have many terms in our language for this: stoned, wired, loaded, blitzed. These terms refer to the body disappearing and the drug or the addiction taking over. One becomes a mass of wires—wired; or one becomes a stone—stoned. The addiction becomes the "active" one, the individual "inactive," passive. He becomes, then, something inanimate, no longer an organic being, but rather a substance, an addiction. He is no longer a man with a life or with relationships.

A bumper sticker meant to be humorous is one which reads, "born to shop." What would it really be like if one really adopted that vision of self—born only to consume, to spend?

Now we know that every human experience has a meaning and a value. Are there ways to understand addiction as something valuable? Is there a way to make sense of the data that show we are a "nation of addicts"? Is there something to be salvaged, transformed, understood about addictions that can help us comprehend the impulse of Mark Hunter, who is after all a very well-meaning, intelligent man wanting to have a decent life?

There is a model for a kind of addiction in traditional religious experience that has a much different intention and flavor, though it retains similarities to what we have been describing as a "problem."

The etymology of the word *addict* is from the Latin "addictus" or "addicere" which means "to award, to assign, or devote": *ad* meaning "to," *dicere* meaning "to say." What this means is "to speak to," in the sense of speaking to a higher power or to strong devotion, to assign value to something higher. The meaning of devotion is to vow or sacrifice or promise oneself solemnly to a deity. So in the concept of addiction, and this had been pointed out by various writers, there is a kind of devotion, self-sacrifice, or solemn promise of some kind. A person becomes selfless as he bows to the "god" cocaine (or any drug/activity) and "devotes" excessive time, money, fantasy, and loyalty to this deity. So addiction means a kind of devotion to something else. This overwhelming desire for selfless devotion somehow gets distorted in the process of being given over to a drug, to a world of consumption, of substance abuse, and self-destruction.

The father's duty is to recognize the incredible responsibility he has to model the importance of devotion to something higher and greater. After all, the young boy is naturally devoted to the father. That is where his "addiction," his vows, his sacrifice of self goes, to his father. The son must be allowed his worship of the father. It is the father's job to know that this is a high honor that he must respect. The father must realize that this devotion is temporary and will be strongly contradicted and broken when the son becomes aware that the father is only human and a real failure as a god. (In our chapter "Father's Body as Challenge," especially the section entitled "Defeat of the Father," you will remember, we discussed the importance and value of this moment we called "father's failure.")

We have written at length about the earliest sense of developing personal power in the growth of a young boy in his relation to his father. The simplest things—things which seem simple to an adult father, that is—can be among the most powerful spiritual experiences for the young boy. It may seem from an adult perspective, cute, funny, or simple for a little boy to run up against his father, to charge against him growling. For the son, it is like running up against the god–father and feeling for a moment his power and strength. The son feels secure and wonderfully safe in his devotion. These experiences that the father helps provide for the son through his personal presence are the very ones he needs throughout life. All men continue to need the presence of their father.

The type and kind of fathering we need at any one time varies some, though certain elements remain constant throughout our lives. In some ways, we always need a father. When we are very young, we need a literal father for very visceral reasons, to establish a core sense of self in the body and in our emotional life. Later we require the mentor to help us know how to feed the mind, the body, and the emotional life, and how to gain a little bit of spiritual food as well. In late life, we most need a kind of relationship with a spiritual father or our own experience of God.

The father uses his body to help the young boy understand how his body works. He sees how it works as a mechanism, as an organism, a physical presence. These are core experiences that can help the boy develop his own personal power, his own sense of personal energy, his understanding that a man's body can be known and trusted; it is OK to be patient with the processes of the body and to develop personal, physical, and emotional security and self-regulation that comes from oneself. He can learn that abuse of artificial, external regulators of the body are unnecessary.

A sense of personal energy is essential for feeling in touch with his inner world and then being able to move out into the world and make a place for himself and his family. And, with this solid foundation, he may later have the strength and desire to develop spiritually.

The absence of a physically and psychologically present father is, in these terms, a deep and permanent personal loss for a boy. Recovery from such a loss, if it comes at all, is slow, painstaking, grievous and difficult. If a young man does not work with and have guidance from an older man to "find himself" as a man, a son, a brother, a disciple, an apprentice, an athlete, and the like, using his natural body, his emotions, his connections with others, his own personal power and energy, he will never be able to move into a truly evolved higher self, a spiritual self. He will always be wondering where his home is and never have a sense of it.

This is, for us, a sad aspect about those who use drugs, who, before they have even had a good sense of feeling at home in their body, create an artificial sense of the body. To use artificial regulation of the body's processes through drugs leaves one homeless. An addicted man asks: What if I don't have my drug? How will I act? What will I do?

When one has learned the art of trusting the body, there is a different sense of one's own rhythms, one's own way of acting and being in the world at home, at work, and in friendships. True, many men were taught distrust of the body. We were taught to believe in using external motivators to drive us or that the "pull" of money or acquisition will help us act. What if we adult men did not have that physically present father as boys? Well, we can certainly grieve that loss. The grief is very important to feel. We need to know that we can work through this grief, and that we can stand it. This is a crucial part of learning self-regulation of the body—that one can move through a difficult experience of pain and sadness. This excruciatingly slow process of recovery helps to salvage our masculine selves. How does one begin such a process? These are questions that we tackle in our chapters on reconciliation.

Chapter 7

Friends and Enemies

Just Other Men

A recent trend suggests that there is something "wrong" with men's friendships—that they are "superficial," work based, activity oriented, and lacking depth and intimacy. In some ways, that can be true. Women's relationships oftentimes are less centered on activities. Their get-togethers usually involve twos and threes, so the groups are a little smaller than men's. In women's friendships, what seems to be of primary importance is the relationship itself, the intimacy and the support that women can share with each other. The relationship is primarily based on feelings, with importance placed on closeness and support.

Men tend to do things in larger groups than women. Their activities together tend to be physical, intense; there is a formal element of competition. These are the trademarks of some types of men's relationships.

Unfortunately, many men today have attempted to understand and define their relationships in the same terms that women define theirs. In other words, women have talked about men's friendships as centering on superficial activity. They often define a "real relationship" as one in which there is "support, intimacy, openness" of a kind that is—at least culturally, in our time—more identified and "natural" for women. This show of support and intimacy that many women learn to express, however, feels less "natural" to men. Yet men have felt that there is something "wrong" with the kind of friendships they have with other men. Many men have developed a self-conscious attitude, even suspicion, toward their desire to have a friendship on the basis of an activity. This attitude promotes a sense of loneliness and insufficiency on the part of men, because they are measuring themselves against the scale of women, against the abilities and talents that many women have for a feminine type of friendship, one based more primarily on feelings. Once you feel insufficient or inadequate in the way you do something, a cycle begins. If you feel inadequate and lonely, you are less likely to want to be action oriented or participate in activities. If you begin to see this as less important or less meaningful—"just" hanging out with the guys, playing basketball, golf, going hunting—then you are looking for the kind of relationship that women you know have with their friends, and you are in for some trouble.

We think that there is something meaningful and vital in the kinds of friendships that men have traditionally had with each other. We are not suggesting that men, in their existing friendships, could not benefit from greater intimacy, greater support among one another, or by adopting, understanding, or developing some of the kinds of traits suggested by the models of women's friendships. What we are saying is that the kinds of relationships that are natural to men have their value, their place, and their meaning, and should be encouraged in whatever form they are taken rather than discouraged, and rejected altogether.

We see trends that women are also attempting to enlarge the framework of their relationships. As men can add the dimension of support and understanding and a base of feeling, women are also finding that there is a vitality that can be injected into their friendships, which comes from more action-oriented activities. We see this in the whole area of exercise, outdoor activities, and sports. Women are shaping a certain amount of their connecting in physical activity, which until the past couple of decades has been a domain more specifically identified with men.

Let's extend this notion of the differences between men and women's friendships to perceptual differences. My wife will oftentimes ask me questions after I have come home from playing baseball or basketball or golf, or having been to a game as a spectator. For example, "What did you talk about?" "Nothing." "You mean you were there with those guys for four hours and nothing of substance came up?" "Well, yes . . . " "What *did* you talk about? You had to say something!" "We talked about baseball."

A woman, talking to an intelligent, otherwise apparently conscious male, who gets this response will be incredulous. That a man could spend this amount of time with other people and not talk about feelings, children, or relationships, that the only thing that came up in eight hours of fishing was, say, what kind of lure to use for largemouth bass on a day like this, is perhaps beyond belief. But the essence of the activity the men are participating in is the main thing. How men talk about breaks in the green or the shortstop shaded toward second comes easy, it comes naturally.

Men in the past spent their days interacting directly with nature, using their bodies in activities in order to survive. Men were hunters and warriors. They collected from the world what was needed to fill the belly and to, well, do something. Roaming out in the world—often silently because it was better that way, in order not to frighten the prey off—is something we still long for, unconsciously and in our deep body tissue. There is a longing in men's bodies and among men for that powerful interaction with the natural world through activity.

Women were until very recently by the hearth or, at farthest, out in the fields by the dwelling, gathering things to eat while the men hunted. Their circle was the domestic place, where they worked hard at preparing food and raising the children. They watched over kids, talked with them, talked with each other, observed each other, supported each other.

Men, when they go out to fish, hunt, play golf, or play baseball, find a reconnection with a mythic and physiological past which cannot be duplicated in the office, factory, or house. It is not that the office, factory, or house are bad, or places to be shunned. But there is an ancient calling in the body to find the activity, the movement, the impact on the natural world that can only be satisfied by doing, working, and moving. Nothing else can satisfy a man in the same way.

A new frame for our understanding of intimacy might be suggested. Two men playing golf together, talking about nothing but the greens, the movement of the ball through the air, the wind, the quality of the course—this is a kind of intimacy in which men are finding themselves in the natural world with each other. There is a quality of intimacy there that is not the same kind of intimacy that women are talking about; it is not the same kind of interior intimacy. But there is an intimacy, in that they are sharing a moment which re-creates or reminds them, even in some small way, of their ancient link with nature in the activity among men. It is a different understanding of intimacy than discussing or expressing feelings with each other; not better, not worse, different—a different frame around the notion of intimacy, connectedness, and understanding. On this level, for example, "support" means men engaging in the same activity together. Even when there is competition between them, there is still an understanding between them in their attempt to have an impact on the world.

Two men fishing together in a boat are attempting to do something that is really quite difficult—catch fish. You may think it is easy to deceive a fish. But it is tough. So two grown men with a lot of world experience do a basic, simple activity—fish together in a boat. They are attempting to reach down into a world they don't understand, and to learn something about it—what will entice and deceive the fish.

This is a kind of intimacy that is worth exploring further. Two people are doing something together, not talking much. What is going on? They may be telling fishing stories while they are fishing. We could understand this as something superficial. But it has an enormous attraction to it for millions of people. Have we missed something important? Perhaps simply being together, experiencing something together, has an intrinsic value that doesn't need a lot of explaining, expression of feelings, or analysis to be of value. It is valuable in itself, and does not require analysis.

Women now are beginning to participate more and more in activities traditionally associated with men. They are coming away from the hearth to the lakes, to the golf courses and softball diamonds, to hiking and biking, to rock climbing, and to the mountains. As women have begun to discover more of the external world and men are working more on discovering their internal world, we are moving to a very exciting meeting place between them.

Now, men can surely benefit from perusing and assessing relationships, looking at what they do and don't have. Once we accept the notion that there is something valuable in the activity orientation, traditional to men's relationships, we have to recognize also that most men in fact are lonely. Part of this loneliness stems from a self-definition and a vision of men's friendships as superficial and inadequate and a vision of men as inadequate. But part of it does, indeed, come from a kind of terror on the part of men to engage in some of the hard work to dig down into their feelings and fantasies, and work on what is "in there."

If you ask them, many men would say that the level and range of their male friendships are limited and unsatisfying. It is not unusual for there to be men who are almost entirely isolated from contact with other men. If you look at the time they spend with people other than at work, they spend it all with women and children. Then there is another group of men who spend some time with men in their extended family. But most men are really, in an essential way, isolated from the world of men. Many do not even attempt to engage in activities with others. Even the activity-oriented men seem to have lost their joy in just doing things as men.

There is a loneliness and alienation that takes place inside a man who has only the company of women and children. Something is lost there for the man who finds himself cut off from other men. Even if their relationships with women fill the need for intimate friendship—since most men find it easier to "open up" to women—they feel something missing if they do not have intimacy with other men. Women, despite any good intentions on their part, cannot fully understand what it is like to be a man (as men cannot do so with women). Something crucial is gained when men can exchange empathy and support with one another.

Many men have felt unsatisfied with their all-male relationships and have looked for depth in a connection with women. This dissatisfaction stems from having blocked intimacy with other men (and in many cases, with women as well). There is room in men's lives for intimate friendships with other men as well as with women. Each friendship offers its own unique rewards, and is to be valued intrinsically.

A couple of steps can be taken to expand the context of men's friendships. One is to have a greater understanding and encourage activities among men as a basis of friendship. A second step is for men to pay attention to the questions, confrontations, and doubts that have been raised by the women's movement and women generally in recent years regarding men's capacity or desire for intimacy. For an enriched experience of friendship, men need to embrace what is natural—the activity base—but also to explore the realms of feelings and intimacy with other men.

Men need to evaluate the quality of the kinds of action-based groupings that they are involved with. Some of them do provide a good sense of camaraderie, good will, and the like, and others do not, even though on the surface it looks as if they do. Some activities with men lose the quality of sharing when the activity is centered around the debasement of women or when the center of activity is dependent upon the use of mind-altering substances. When the activity is centered on those two kinds of structures, there is little possibility of intimacy.

Another thing that is problematic in many culturally acceptable male group activities is that the focus is often totally or primarily on competition and precision. What gets lost is the sharing of the atmosphere, like the current in the stream or the fog in the morning as you move out into the field or the lake. Instead, the focus is on the number of fish you get, the number of ducks shot, the score in the game, or who won and who lost. We don't mean that these factors should not be a part of the situation, because there is a certain excitement only competition can bring. Competition can ignite an intensity that can be very satisfying. But when the activity is focused entirely on the outcome, who is better or more proficient, to that extent there is something lost between men.

Many women seem to create continuity in their relationships across time. Some men have been able to incorporate this value, but a good many men do not. If work is the only way that they connect, then men are exposed to only task-related relationships, which may end with a job transfer. What they then lack is that sense of depth and continuity that enables a friend to pick up with someone, though months or years have elapsed. Many women know what it is like to be in a friendship for a long time. This is an area that women seem to maintain a lot better than men and men could learn something from them.

In times of significant stress in the lives of men, the lack of depth and continuity in the friendships of men hits home. In other words, if your friendships are totally activity based, when you really need support or encouragement with regard to changes, stresses, and difficulties in life, you won't find it there. We all hit these points more often than we'd like to admit. Most men simply have not learned to relate on the level of deep feelings, or to ask for support. Many even refuse to acknowledge the impact of changes on their lives.

When a man's best and only friend is his wife, however, and he is cut off from other men or only interacts with them in terms of work or hobbies, he can feel very lonely. If that primary relationship is ruptured in some way, he can feel even worse, since he has not worked at a connection with other men and can't get male support during this time of pain and change. The most abiding and powerful model for a connection between males on the level of deep feelings is the relationship with one's father and one's son.

In our chapter on reconciliation with the father, we focus on the preparation needed before the son can connect with his father or the father with his adult son. This preparation—internal preparation and expression of old wounds, griefs, pain—is necessary not only for a relationship with your father, but to foster a compassion for other men who are themselves sons and fathers. By connecting to the experiences of loss, grief, and pain, as well as the joy that can be felt when reconciling with your father, you can draw on these feelings when interacting with other men. Through this preparation, you can expand the experience of yourself as a male.

A man in one of our men's groups, Fred, is a stock analyst for a large national corporation. He came to therapy because of an enduring hostility and resentment toward his father, who continued (though Fred was forty-three years old) to tell his son who to associate with in business, who his friends should be, and how he should invest his money. Over the past several months, Fred has told the group about his feelings of humiliation and anger at his father, and has been able to feel the understanding and support of other group members. He can now speak with his father over the phone without becoming infuriated, and at times will initiate a call to his father himself. With group support and understanding, Fred has been able to recognize and appreciate his own competence, and to tell his father directly that he will choose friends and investments on the basis of his own judgment, and that he wants friendship rather than advice from his father. The two of them have been getting along well recently. Also, Fred has noticed that he feels more relaxed and competent at work, that he has made more time to be with his wife and children, and that he has struck up a friendship with a man he knows from a church group.

A reconciliation with your father will naturally begin to enrich, inform, and deepen your experience of your work, your activities, your relationships with other men. Reconnection with old wounds and pain, and with your father both as he is today and as he once was, is the door which opens onto relationships with other men on a deeper level.

To allow others to know you in this way is to bring a new continuity to your sense of self. This understanding of your pain allows you to begin to talk with other men about the losses, the problems, the deepest emotions of your life. This enables you to experience compassion for other men's grief, which in turn diminishes the need for competition. This also diminishes loneliness and increases your capacity for intimacy.

Work relationships and play relationships contain inherent value which can be enhanced by emotional connection. This connection through feeling begins in its primary form with your father. The relative level of closeness or distance with your father has a dramatic impact on the figure you cut in the world at large and your relations with other people, specifically with other men. Without father–son closeness in childhood, a man feels uncomfortable, afraid, and unworthy of closeness with other men. Without that closeness, you will likely hold back from other men. This will literally increase your isolation and lead to the thoughts that other men are frightening and mysterious. You will think of other men as strangers and yourself as a stranger to them. If your connection with other men is shallow, you are likely to create only a thin veneer of social skills in order to relate to other men; but, essentially, you will never know them and they will never know you. You may have a lingering fear that connecting with other men would be strange, uncomfortable, and only net you more grief; thus, this connection is to be bypassed at all costs. But have heart. You can change and learn to understand yourself and other men better, and increase your trust with them and with yourself.

One thing that fathers can certainly do for their sons and that can have reverberations in the future generations is to offer a model for relating to men. Sons watch their fathers and learn how they connect with other men. Whether the son is ever drawn into connecting with other men will be very significantly influenced by this model.

A very enjoyable thing I did as a boy was to caddy for my father when he played golf. It was an honor and privilege for me to do this, because I was included like an apprentice with my father and his friends. It gave me an idea of what my father was like around other men. I could observe him with his friends, with the "guys." I liked seeing how they were together and I liked his friends; they treated me well, and I felt I was being included among the men.

When a father doesn't have good relationships with other men, this communicates a model of distance and isolation to son. It seems to indicate to the son that he will not be able to have good relationships with men either. He doesn't often get to see his dad operating in a variety of arenas with others like him; he sees him only at home or once in a while on a family trip interacting with other men. But he doesn't see his dad spending time interacting with other men on a regular basis, responding to other men, talking about them, showing his feelings or discussing his thoughts or concerns about his friends. It is very hard for a boy to learn compassion without some training from his father or other men.

I remember once when my dad was with some other men. I heard him use the word *fuck* for the first time. I was an adolescent and had heard the word many times before, of course, but never from him. I had always thought of him as a person who didn't curse or didn't get very angry. He was angry about something, I don't remember what, but the other men were angry about it too, and were all expressing their anger. Then I remember that they started deciding what they were going to do about the situation, but I was in a kind of trance. I was staring at my father, smiling but shocked at the same time. He picked up on my looking at him in that way, and so did the other men. They stopped what they were doing for a moment. He looked at me, as did the other men. He said, "You are surprised I would say such a word, or be so angry, aren't you? Well, it's time you learned that your dad is just an ordinary human being, just like you." The other men smiled at that, and then they all went back to their discussion.

A son needs opportunities to see his father as a human being, a man just like other men, who needs understanding, friendship, support, and compassion.

Looking back over what we have said about men and their friendships with other men, there are several points we would like to underscore here.

First, men need to realize the inherent differences in the way they relate to other men and the way women relate to each other. There is something wonderful, vital, mysterious, and meaningful about the way men spend time together. What men have is not inferior, but rather, special and very distinct from what women have. Second, men can enlarge the framework of the relationships they have with other men. A movement toward depth, support, and shared feelings with other men can be a crucial part of a man's sense of his maleness and humanity. Relationships which have these components in them are to be sought and treasured. Third, for sons to get a good idea of how to relate to other men, fathers of young sons need first to evaluate their own relationships with other men. Often, they can improve the quality of their relationships and attempt to deepen areas of their lives as men, for themselves and for their sons. Intergenerational connections are essential. Whenever possible, you should encourage your son in the development of peer relationships, but also in those vital connections with the men of the family, the men of your blood history.

Perhaps the most important thing we would encourage fathers and adult sons to do is the difficult work of reconciling with your own father. In taking the risk of exposing yourself to this process, you will inevitably find grief and pain. That is the bad news. The good news is that once a reconciliation has taken place internally, whether it takes place externally or not, you will begin to experience a greater level of confidence in yourself, as well as acceptance, compassion, and the discovery of something that was there all along: the longing to be in the company of the community of men.

With the confidence you may find a real qualitative difference in the relationships you have with other men. The competition, the dominance–submission patterns that have overshadowed your relationships in the past may begin to change to richer and less stereotyped ways of relating. You will also understand more about why competition, though significant and meaningful, is only valuable in limited ways, to the extent that it sharpens experience, but that taken too far, it deadens your enjoyment in life. You will be less likely, with your increased sense of confidence, to let yourself be victimized by the drive to compete. You don't have to kill or smash down your father or other men once you have a greater sense of compassion for yourself and for them.

Chapter 8

Sons Adrift in the Workplace

Work has become more abstract in modern society. It is especially hard for young children to grasp what a parent does at work, where a parent goes, and how well the parent does at his or her occupation. It is very difficult for the young son to grasp any idea about what the father is like in a very important sphere of his adult life. Is his father in charge of other people, is he a father for them, too? Does he get along with other coworkers? How does he solve problems? Does he seem comfortable and happy with his job? In effect, the son has little or no information about how the father functions in the work world. What a son misses is the immediate body rhythms, the movements of his father at work. He has no conception of how the father uses his body, his senses, at work. How does he use his hands? What about his feet? His breathing?

It is one thing for a young man to hear about a job, or to be told how a job is done. In college one may be given a description of what a job requires, what the intellectual requirements are, and what background is needed. For example, in engineering, a student may learn how to devise a plan or a structure, and how to conceive the way that a job can be done: its math, its drawings, the job-bidding process, and the politics. It is another thing to be in the presence of a master of a particular kind of work, to see, hear, and witness the various ways the master actually does the work—to see how a senior engineer goes about synthesizing information, intuition, and activity. What does he do first? How does he move? What are his rituals? What does he pick up first? Does he work at a fast pace, or slowly and methodically?

The actual experience of work is something very remote from a young man's vision of entering the working world. He has not, in most cases, been near or with his father or other adult male, to get a sense of what it is like to "be at work." Even if he has a good understanding of the father's work, not knowing what it feels like to be around that kind of workplace is a loss.

Even perhaps more basic than not having had the experience of working side by side and watching the father or "master," is the fact that many children have never even visited the father's workplace at all. There is a need for boys (and girls), a fundamental need, to have a sensate image of the father between the time he leaves for work and the time he returns home. The son needs to be able to situate the father, to place him somewhere in his own mind. It helps if the son has actually visited the father's place of work, and has a visual, auditory, and kinesthetic feel or image of the environment in which the father works. This is one way that some of this lost sense of time, the absence of the father, and the connection between son and father can be addressed.

I am remembering a scene from the movie *Kramer versus Kramer*, when the son is quite distanced from the father and they have to forge a relationship of some kind because they are going to be alone for the first time without the mother's presence. After awhile, the son finally visits where the father works. It is way up in the sky and has huge windows. The son is quite taken with the view, but also the easels there. He begins to get a picture of his father as an artist, one who puts things together, who paints, pastes, who works with his hands and creates images. It is noteworthy that this scene occurs at this particular point in the film, because it coincides with the father and son beginning to come together for the first time.

Another thing that a young son needs, but that a lot of people miss throughout life, is an essential lesson in the meaning of work. This is the experience of pleasure, the pleasure that can be part of work. If a boy never sees his father at work, and only experiences his father being grouchy in the morning getting ready for work and tired in the evening, he begins to form a picture that work is an unpleasurable experience, something at best just required of someone, at worst, an evil, painful experience. Even though the father may have a pleasurable experience at work, a kind of rhythm of excitement and involvement in connections with others, the son may mistake the "daily bitching" as a sign that work is a grim necessity. He will miss observing dad stretch his arms, pull up his shirt sleeves and generate the energy and motivation needed to meet the challenges of the day. Even if the father works at a job which he doesn't like, he might focus on the positive aspects of his job. For example, an assembly-line worker can focus on showing his son the product that gets manufactured and on his coworkers.

Unfortunately, many have come to associate the rewards of work as being almost entirely connected with the paycheck that comes with the job. Isn't it a sad thing that many people spend the most productive time of most of their days doing something that they conceive of as pleasureless, joyless, and without excitement?

When we ask people, especially men, what they conceive of as play or fun, most of them answer with some form of childish experience, something having to do with drinking, watching football games, or "doing nothing." "What I would really like to do is just do nothing. Sit on the beach, drinking margaritas." How rare that experience would be for most people, and how unfulfilling for some people when it does happen, particularly if they are returning after a week of leisure to a job in which they have found little value. One of the most disappointing times in some people's lives is when they go on vacation and realize the emptiness of "vacating." Yet, returning to work is seen by most people as a painful experience because they have not found pleasure in their work, but at least they are returning to a familiar ritual.

Fathers need to pass the value of work on to their sons, not only the values of completing a job well done or productivity. But the father needs to communicate to his son the definition of work as part of a commitment to life. How does the father see work as an extension of his place in life, as well as his place in the world? Where does he sit in the scheme of things, and how does his work reflect his values? What vision does he have of himself as a "worker?"

Many have lost a sense of the value of work as a pleasurable and meaningful experience. In addition to monetary rewards, it is important to see work as a use of oneself, as a valuable use of one's own energy, body, and time. Few (probably no) forms of work are innately without meaning or value. However, it is true that any job can be done with a mean, dispirited attitude, one which encourages the view of work as something ugly and disliked. All work has rewards. We may think of aesthetic rewards, that is, what sense of beauty is contributed by my work and products or even through the very rhythms and movements I engage in. Psychological rewards have to do with one's own connection with others and one's connection with self in the workplace. What are my relationships with others like at work? How does this work and the way I do this work affect my view of myself, my self-esteem, and my view of humanity? Emotional rewards are felt in having spent time in a meaningful way as well as interacting with valued company. Spiritual rewards have to do with serving something or someone greater than oneself. In old-fashioned terms, they come from a vocation or a calling to a particular kind of work that makes use of the talents of the individual. The philosopher Paul Weiss writes:

> All wholehearted immersion in work, since it leads to the subjugation of oneself to the processes and structures of Nature, is a way of acting in accordance with the rhythms of Existence. He who acts in this way submits himself and his interests, his efforts, and the value of his work to Existence, is thereby able to face God in a dynamic relation to himself. (p. 316).

What Weiss is saying is something very different from the point of view that work is something done to puff up one's own ego or one's sense of private, personal power. When Weiss talks about immersing oneself, subjugating oneself within the work, he is deepening our understanding, opening up our view of a "calling" to work.

The father communicates to his son a meaning to life by embodying a sense that work epitomizes one type of relationship with the world, a way of using one's own body, one's own energy, and one's own time to create value and beauty through activity. In his most basic activities, such as in work, in providing for himself and for the family, the father models his view of the universe, how the universe is according to him. If he goes off to work in a begrudging and grouchy manner, what he communicates to his son is that the world is not a worthwhile place, that the rhythms of daily life, his body, his nature, are unacceptable to him. He says, in effect, that his view of himself and his efforts, as well as those of other men around him, are to little purpose or meaning. What son is going to respect or enjoy work and purposeful action in the world, if this is the model he comes to adopt?

Here are some questions for you to consider about your own work patterns, views about work, and experiences with your father related to work:

- What do you see as the value and purpose of work? Is work only a way to make money, a necessary evil, a way to serve others, a way to find meaning in life?
- Is your work enjoyable to you? When during your work life have you found enjoyment or pleasure in something you are doing? Is that happening now? How do you explain this?
- Does your work fit with your values? Is what you do consistent with your moral standards?
- Can you remember working with your father on any work project? What did you do and what did he do? Was it enjoyable or drudgery?
- Did your father teach or instruct you as you worked together? Were you thanked or praised for your efforts? If you were, how did you feel about that? If not, what did you feel?
- What is your current experience of working with men older than you or younger than you are?

- Do you and your father ever do any work together now? If so, how is that for you? Is it enjoyable, productive, strained? Do old frustrations surface as each of you compete for who is in charge or knows more? If not, imagine that you are working together and how you think that would be for you.
- Have you been involved in a work project in which three or four generations of men participated, such as restoring or building a house, working in a garden, cutting a Christmas tree, or other project? If so, what was the scene like for you? If not, imagine a scene like this in your family, and what you think it would be like.

In earlier chapters, we spoke of the father's body as a kind of "womb," "shield," or "mechanism." These images are very powerfully portrayed in the way the father works and the attitude he conveys toward work. What he communicates to his son about basic values toward the universe—through the manner in which he conducts himself—leaves more of a long-lasting impression on the son than any words can express.

For a father today who may not have the opportunity to work side by side with his son on a daily basis, there are still opportunities for them to join forces in activities that are still defined as work; yard work, cutting wood, planting, painting, repairing, building, writing letters. These are all activities that permit father and son to work side by side in cooperation and apprenticeship. For example, my three-year-old son enjoys helping me make fires. He delights in gathering wood and helping me arrange it in the fireplace. It is an activity that we do together, and that I see him imitate in other aspects of his playtime in terms of "being a firebuilder."

Another thing that is rare in the workplace today is the sense of the "old master," the mentor, figuring prominently in the daily life of the working man. Frank, for example, is a corporate executive in one of the large companies in our town. He was complaining to me that there are no mentors in his corporation. He is thirty-seven years old and he says that all of the people he works with, even those in fairly high management positions, are between thirty-five and forty-five years old. He feels like his days are spent among "boys" and without a full sense of accomplishment, even though he does his job well. He wants to have the opportunity of working with a master, learning his rhythms and the masterful way he'd do the job. Frank regrets that he has no access to mentors. The oldest person in Frank's corporation is fifty-five years old and he has no access to him anyway. Frank imagined what it would be like with older mentors on board: "How good it would be to go around with the old masters, side by side, and to spend the day with them and see how they go about their life and talk with them and get ideas, information, and possibilities from those patriarchs, those fathers who have been through so much in life. We weed everybody out the instant their hair gets thin or they start getting a little reflective or slower, a little quieter or just a little less peppy!" He said that his job seems at times like continuing college throughout life. He spends almost all of his time with people his own age. Even though he knows he is doing a good job, he still feels a keen sense of fatherlessness, the lack of a deep layer of experience within the corporation.

Isn't this a very common experience in our companies? As people approach retirement age, they are no longer seen as prime property within corporations; they are seen as fading out, expensive, and easily replaceable. This is a travesty in our work world. It creates a fatherlessness, ahistorical feel in the workplace. There is often no one to carry the history and experience of humble beginnings and glorious triumphs. There is no living, breathing tradition in many of our corporations.

When you have older men working in the company, what gets added in the experience is something more than product, more than outcome. They confer onto the company a sense of history and continuity, which adds a solidity and a sense of substance to the job and to what one represents. They also imbue a corporation with a sense of spirit and humanity. Have you noticed how the papers often record the death of the last member of a championship sports team? They comment that an era is ending, and with it a connection to pride and tradition.

Many people today are intolerant of old age, diversity, and personal idiosyncrasies within the workplace. When I was teaching, years ago, I started in a private high school. There were a number of teachers, older teachers, who were quirky, odd, unusual men. They represented for kids and also for other teachers the possibility of being different, of living life in ways other than in the very narrow band of acceptability. One, Roger, was a man dedicated to eighteenth-century British literature and to working for Amnesty International. Given to wearing unfashionable baggy clothes, he would mutter to himself, and rarely attend staff meetings; if he did, it was to attack the pettiness of the administration. A certain core group of extremely creative young men gathered around him year after year. I know of at least three fine authors that came out of Roger's "entourage." He was finally asked to "retire early" when a new headmaster decided that he didn't like Roger's attitude, the fact that he would not wear a necktie, and that he "incited students." I would rather say that he "insighted students," which is apparently a dangerous thing to do.

Several teachers "fell" in the late seventies, when the new educational trend, the push for more "quantitative measurement" in education (whatever that might mean), developed. These older teachers, many of whom had a real sense of human experience and sense of their subject—not just of the content but a love and passion for their subject (which may have little to do with quantitative learning)—were able to instill in their students a lifelong passion for their subjects. Because this was their focus and they refused to change their humanistic attitude, several of these teachers ended up taking "early retirement" or were simply asked to leave. Very soon the school began to be a homogeneous group of demanding, young to middle-aged teachers who required the kids to perform over and over again certain quantitative tasks. The kids got a lot better at taking exams. Oddly enough, the enrollment began to drop off. I wonder why? Perhaps it was simply a matter of demographics, of fewer young people available to fill the classes. However, I think—I am being naive here, of course—that they missed that sense of variety, oddness, humanity, the sense that education had to do with bringing oneself out of oneself. A prep school was really supposed to be about going head to head with teachers about basic philosophies of life, challenging life or world view against world view.

What the old teachers were trying to communicate is that there is something greater than the ego, something greater than passing examinations. They saw that the purpose of life is to find your own way, and your own understanding of your small place within it. Once these teachers left, something was lost in the environment of the school; it lost its pervasive sense of humanity, and the quirky, odd ways of the old teachers, which will be a long time returning. We have been steadily losing fathers through this century. More and more they are being replaced with buffed and polished wiseguys, middle-aged performance maniacs.

Now, achievement is all important. Production is all important. These goals help the practical survival and give a push to the material commerce of our world. However, many men are beginning to question these ends in themselves and to seek work and work environments which have an element of pleasure and value in them. Though several generations of men have worked joylessly as automatons, a new man is emerging who does not accept work or workplaces which are joyless. This is not immaturity, but a new and higher definition of maturity, a desire for good, hard work which is also done with delight and in the quest for higher values, perhaps spiritual ones.

Men have historically linked their adequacy and their worth with performance and accomplishment. Clearly there are positive aspects to that. However, for a good many men, working hard, late hours is being used as an escape from intimacy with family and friends. In some cases, they are enjoying their coworkers and view them as their primary supportive friends. However, it can be defense which attempts to cover a marginal sense of being at home in the world, a loss of connection with other people or themselves. If you work long hours away from your family or away from free time with friends, you may want to look at the focus of this expenditure of time. Is it rewarding and meaningful to you to be at work? Is it worth the cost to your family life? Are you avoiding your family?

Work can become an obsessive and preoccupying search which men hope (often in vain) will mirror back to them that there is something essentially right, good, and solid about themselves. One of the worst parts of this search and this clawing for an illusion is that because it is compelling and preoccupying, it isolates the man. It cuts him off from his family, his inner life, his son. It cuts him off from his essential humanity.

Art was co-owner of an electrical contracting firm. For the past thirty-five years he has worked over sixty hours a week. Though he is a fine worker, his obsession with work has left him distant from his wife and family, and with few outside interests. He has taken only two vacations during his work life, one to Hawaii and one to Mexico, and slept during most of the time during these trips. As he approaches retirement age, Art is becoming depressed and despondent, and the quality of his work has declined noticeably. Work appears to be his whole identity at this point, and he sees little of value or interest in the years ahead of him.

Work need not be a source of alienation from intimacy. The courageous man, the courageous father, is beginning to realize that he has a right to the "pursuit of life, liberty, and happiness," that he need not be a robot. For a mature man, work should be an element of his happiness and his liberty and his life. A dedication to the search for joy and meaning in your labor is a sign of your maturity—and is a priceless heirloom for your son.

Chapter 9

The Absent Man

Riddles of Men and Women

Women are often puzzled and amazed as they watch their lovers and husbands wallow around, crash, and bumble in their relationships. They watch men they know compete with their fathers and yet try to please them. These men feel rejected or cut off from their fathers, friends, from themselves—and from women. Women look on with horror and astonishment as their husbands or lovers muck around with their own sons and compete with them, try to control and criticize, or attempt to mold them in some kind of image. This is painful for the women as well as the men. It is awkward for women as they try to discover what their role is in these situations, what they should do, and how they can help these men mend fences and find ways to communicate with each other. Women themselves also struggle with how to establish a relationship with these befuddled creatures.

One of the things women find themselves doing is operating in the role known as "mediator." They find that they are the peacemakers between their husbands and their husband's father or between son and father. They buffer, they soothe, they translate; they are the primary persons who decipher communications. What that creates is ongoing problems for men with "mother in the middle." All parties remain in fixed roles. The woman acts as peacemaker between father and son, who will not speak civilly to each other. Problems don't get solved, communication does not improve, and distance is never bridged. It is as awkward for the mother to find her way with her sons and her husband as it is for them to find their way with each other and with her.

One of the difficulties in the relationship between a woman and a man arises when the man has not resolved his relationship with his father. As we've noted before, he then becomes stuck finding his way into manhood, and into his own maturity. He may not have committed himself to a kind of work, to the role of being a father; he may not have found comfort, excitement, and interest in work or in friendships with other men; and he may be using forms of addiction to avoid facing the process of "growing up."

Oftentimes we see adult sons who have arrested their development somewhere in adolescence. Many women have done much work in recent years on their own maturity, developing a psychological awareness of their inner life, that is, in finding their way in the world. Many women who have had to struggle to find a position in the world of men and in the work world, including the economic world, have fought very hard against odds to get a place of respect. It makes sense for women to lose respect for men who won't take their own place or work hard to become mature, or who shirk from confronting their inner selves.

There is a kind of man who stays young and uncommitted and is afraid to enter the world. Many women see these men as incompetent; yet, we often see women waiting for the men in their lives to become someone they don't seem ready to become yet. A lot of men and women seem frozen in this position of the man being reluctant to mature and the woman being the driving force, and yet very dissatisfied with him. Women rightfully have complained about this sort of incompetence in men. The problem with this frustration and resentment is that this attitude can often trigger the effect of a man digging deeper into his incompetence.

Many men, having gotten little from their fathers, have relied almost entirely on their mother's praise and support—they have not experienced this kind of attention from men. They are now looking for the kind of praise and support they got from mother from a woman who is wife, lover, or friend. Rightfully so, women are becoming less willing to be the mothers to these incompletely developed males. So there exists a circle of incompetence, disrespect, and resentment that develops between men and women which turns round and round, endlessly.

Many men find that they are incapable of pleasing their father, their wives, their children, and that only mother still seems to be pleased with them. What they need is a resolution with father (and other men), the attention of other men, and recognition of their talents and worth by men. Only this can help a man find his way to the lost part of his maturity (along with a spiritual life, which must come after the development of a solid relationship with other men).

In this chapter, we make suggestions for women (and for men about how to inform women in their lives) concerning how to live with the adult son/father who has chosen the difficult road of reconciliation with his father/son and other men. We also discuss how to support him and live with him through these times as he is working through a difficult period.

Women who identify so thoroughly with a mothering role not only do it with their own children but also with husbands, friends, and lovers. Instead of creating a stronger bond between the two of them, this kind of woman actually weakens it. As the woman "mothers" more and more and as the adult son experiences that relationship primarily as a maternal one, the man's personal competence begins to suffer—which in turn seems to cry out for a greater level of caretaking. The couple's sex life begins to dry up; the man begins to experience his lover no longer as a viable sexual partner.

Essentially, what a man has learned about himself has come from a woman and not from men, so a boy has learned what it is like to be a male from the one parent willing to talk to him—mom. His image of manhood is from the female perspective, and oftentimes dad will be portrayed as inconsequential, uninvolved, and unemotional. The qualities that please the mother most about a male make up a centerpiece around which the young male develops. What is important to the mother is that there be a sensitive, pleasing, civilized son who may be a confidant for her in her times of trouble.

Thus, absence of the father not only has an impact for the son, but also for mother, who misses the company of her husband. What then happens is that the son, as he grows up, begins to adapt the idea that works so well with his mother, his girlfriends, or his wife. It does work well to a certain extent, doesn't it? Women do like the consideration, sensitivity, sharing, and warmth that comes at the beginning of the relationship; why not? But then something changes, and the man becomes resentful about "being good for mom" and then shuts up and is reactive or unresponsive. What women wish for later in the relationship is a certain level of excitement, earthiness, strength, a certain type of power that is lacking in a good number of men.

Of course, a large number of men react to all this neediness on the part of their mothers from the beginning, and they shut her out and decide that women are something akin to black widow spiders, who suck the life blood out of their mates and annihilate them. These men will always keep a distance from women, and will often be abusive and cruel. But they too have learned the lessons of the mother, and know how to be charming and seductive with women, and often have the kind of disdainful Don Juan charm and excitement, lacking in the soft gooey man, that is alluring and intriguing. This says something about the enigma of why so many intelligent, seemingly mature women are drawn into involvement with men they know (on some level) will be abusive toward them.

A solid kind of strength, earthiness, joy, and sexual energy—rather than a false machismo—comes from a man's connection with his body and with his maleness. This cannot develop in the same way with a woman that it can in his relationships with men, and in particular in his connection with his father. A man cannot develop a masculine strength and ability to meet the world solely from the eyes, the vision, of a woman. Father must be visibly and forcefully present.

Absent fathers also offer poor models on how to treat women and how to act in a relationship. There are occasions when the father displays his attitude toward women, such as when he comes home from work or gets up in the morning or is home on weekends. Still, there is no ongoing sense of how father and mother relate with each other.

You can think about your own experience, your own background. How did your father and mother relate to each other? What was your father's attitude toward your mother? Can you trace it—or do you find yourself talking only in vague niceties, "Oh, they got along OK"? Can you think about whether you were taught a kind of fear and avoidance (through father's model) of mother and her attitudes and her criticisms? Were you taught a kind of respect or disrespect for women? As you think about your father and mother living together, did you see a model of cooperation or was it more a model of fighting, a battle of competition and distance? Was there a sense that one would generally lose and one would generally win? Did your father tend to ignore your mother, or was he perhaps overly attentive to her? This sense of the timing and rhythms of the relationship between men and women will be carried by the son into adult life. Whether he carries an image of reciprocal support, marital conflict, or dominance/submission will in large part be influenced by how his parents treated each other.

One thing about the preceding questions that should be clarified is that such things are almost never discussed by men with each other, or in families. The cues, the models, and the directives are given—generally—much more subtly than by direct statement. If you had trouble answering those questions, or the answers seem inconclusive or confusing to you, it is likely that your information was received indirectly and is primarily working on you unconsciously. You might try this exercise.

Imagine that you are alone with your father and looking very carefully at him. In fact, you have a VCR camera recording the interaction, so you can go back and run the scene in slow motion or stop action. Bring up your mother's name and some piece of information about her (perhaps some success she has had, a discussion that you had with her, something about an illness of hers, etc.). Look at your father's face, his eyes, his posture, his gestures; look carefully. What is his tone of voice like (disregarding the words or content)? Does he look excited, interested, involved; or defeated, collapsed, deflated; or angry, stiff, tight; or neutral, disinterested, distant? Now go back two paragraphs and ask the same questions based on what you observed. Now go through the same exercise, but substitute your mother. Bring up something about your father. Look carefully, record the interactions, and then go back to the other questions.

Responses by men to these questions have shown us some noticeable trends. First and foremost is the absence of any clear guide for most males on how to enter and actively participate in the emotional life of the family. Often, fathers are good businessmen and providers, perhaps competent decision makers for the family, but seem frustrated with managing feelings and impatient with the emotional needs of women and children. Second, most men still view women as idealized objects or as sexual objects. The sexual revolution and the women's movement have done very little to change this. The reason for this is that most men have not talked with other men or developed with other men an understanding or way of working with and understanding their relationships with women. In fact, we believe that men are now driven deeper into unconsciousness, and more confused, reactive, and resistant to relationships with women than before these changes. More dissatisfaction with men voiced on the part of women, coupled with less discussion by men with each other for support and "toleration," as well as absent fathering have all contributed to this unconsciousness. We know that men have increasingly used addictions to buffer the pain of this sense of chaos in their role. Addiction becomes the confidant of the father as opposed to closeness with spouse and children. It is an attempt to avoid the pain of connecting in relationships one does not know how to handle.

Fathers and men who have influence with boys and

younger men should know about their impact on them. You can help these young males avoid getting stuck in these traps by setting an example, through talking with them, by spending time with them, and by introducing them to other positive male role models. Your role is crucial in their lives. A father's absence and a mother's dominance may make that mother's son morbid, so intensely so that the son remains the primary confidant and caretaker of the mother. Thus, the intensity and loyalty can stay tied up with mother, which means the kid never grows into adult malehood. You can find this happening often when adult sons talk to their mothers. How often does contact occur and what demands of time and energy are made on him? Will he be likely to fix things over at mom's house before he will fix things at home? Will he avoid his wife and family as his father managed to limit contact?

A couple, Phil and Laurie, came in for therapy with me. They have been married for six years. In the past six months, Phil has become demanding, irritable, and yet uncommunicative about what he is feeling or thinking. There is a growing distance between them. Phil has been spending more and more time at his mother's house, where he is remodeling a kitchen for her, and installing new wiring in the second floor.

Laurie said that they have not had sex for months and she feels like his roommate. At a work-related party, she saw Phil flirting with a woman he works with. He insisted that he is not having a sexual affair with her, but admitted to spending a number of evenings in her company, and even sharing a room in a motel on a recent business trip. When asked by Laurie which of the two he wants to be with, Phil stated that he needs both women while he is "finding himself."

Laurie said that she would not be willing to be married to Phil under these conditions, and that she would be filing for divorce. Phil became enraged and yelled at her in a bellowing voice that she never gives him anything. He proclaimed that all women are demanding and manipulative and that he is "tired of being taken advantage of." Yet, he never really talked with Laurie about what he was feeling or thinking, never really gave her a chance to understand him, nor tried to understand her position. He only came to therapy to try to appease her, yet held a grudge against her for even suggesting that something might be wrong with him or with their marriage.

There is a strong, though often hidden, desire that remains in every man to find his masculinity—to find a definition and understanding of masculinity. Often, the aggression, power, strength, and potency latent in men is not given a kind of direction and instruction on its use, especially in relationships with women.

What we find is men who either overuse or underuse their power. In the case of the overuse of "power" (it is not really potency, but has to do with fantasized "control"), what we find is men who engage in womanizing and trophy hunting with women in the attempt to practice a kind of domination or power over that which is female, just as they felt dominated by their mother. This is an attempt by men to find a way of expressing masculinity; but the harm that has been done from this attitude is immense. It is critical to realize that men who have such an attitude toward women lack an understanding of a properly directed masculine power. The attempt to control or subordinate women is essentially an infantile masculinity. It is not a masculinity that has a balance or certainty to it, but rather that of the enraged, narcissistic infant who wants to tear mom apart because he didn't get what he wanted at the exact moment he wanted it. From that infantile position there is a desire to control a woman in the same way that a young infant tries to control the activity of his mother. As an adult, he then treats women in much the same way. The woman is there in order to meet his needs and demands, not her own. There is little comprehension of a need for any kind of reciprocity in the relationship, that the man must also give something if he is to get something in return.

The other side of this spectrum is the man who underuses his potency or subordinates his masculinity to the point where it nearly disappears, by deciding to have no life of his own apart from women. He lives for "pleasing mother." This can be seen when men are passively involved in the decisions in a relationship, where men don't take a stand, and where they don't express themselves. They are "undercharged," and don't push at all with their potency, but keep it all bottled up. A number of women complain about men today being wimpy or too soft or too gentle. This is not a complaint about the sensitivity of men but a complaint about the men's lack of connection to their masculinity, to their own authority, and to their own sense of discipline and strength.

Joel is a twenty-six-year-old law student, living at his parents' house while working on his degree. He is a pleasant young man, respectful, obedient, and well mannered. Yet, despite these positive qualities, something is missing in him; he has subordinated his own sense of self by complying with his mother's wishes and desires. On a night when extended family came together for his birthday, he demonstrated this vividly. His uncle returned to the house after the party to deliver a present he had forgotten to give his nephew. Joel's mother demanded that he come down and thank his uncle for the present. Joel responded from upstairs, saying that he was in his undershorts, getting ready for bed. His mother told him that it didn't matter what he was doing, he needed to come down and personally thank the gift giver and hug him. Joel put his clothes on quickly, came downstairs with apologies for his slowness, and profusely thanked his uncle for the gift and for coming to his house to celebrate his birthday. He expressed no anger then or afterward at his mother for being so invasive and inconsiderate of him.

At twenty-six years of age, Joel is still subordinating his life to his mother's wishes. When or how will he leave home to establish his own life? Will he be able to express his needs any more clearly to another woman than he currently can with his mother? Will he be potent in the courtroom and impotent at home? As yet, these questions remain unanswered. However, we are concerned for Joel and for other men like him, and for the women they choose to be in relationships with.

Women can live more effectively with the men they have chosen if they can define their own role as woman, mother, wife, lover, confidante, friend, and so on, and be able to relate to the men in their lives in ways that are appropriate. They can help them become more of a self and not less of a self. And they can refuse to rescue men from their own difficulties regardless of how tough things are for them.

First, a woman must look at her own sense of what it is to be a grown woman and what she responds to in a man. Second, she needs to identify what it is to be a mother and whose mother she is (as well as the relationship with her own mother). An old joke is that a woman, when asked, "How many children do you have?" responded, "Three, my two little ones and that big baby, my husband." A woman needs to clarify whose mother she is, continue taking care of herself, and stop taking care of men in ways that diminish her and the men in the process.

There are all kinds of incompetencies that men take on that women will take over and "fix." A vivid example is that of a man who seems to be often "between careers," when his wife drudges away, or, sometimes, gets really involved in a career, but doesn't demand the same from him. In all kinds of ways, for all kinds of reasons, the lover or husband is simply "not able to find the right work."

Anthony has been married to Liz for eight months. Prior to their marriage he was not working and now has just taken a part-time position. He has shown little motivation for making a career choice, preferring to live in the house of and on the paycheck of his executive wife. Though she refused, he requested that they file a joint tax return, with any liability paid by Liz.

As long as the woman continues to take care of the man by providing spending money and a roof over his head, that man will not find a place for himself in the world. Nobody gains. She reinforces his incompetency. This incompetency breeds a level of discontent in the man and he becomes less potent in numerous ways, including sexually. Sometimes he is not interested sexually in his wife or is looking "elsewhere." Now this example is vivid and clear, but the same thing is going on widely in relationships where the man—though he might have a steady job—still whines and complains his way through his days. He never gets his inner life and his work world to meet each other. He just frets and stews while she goes off to work, shuts up, and works hard.

Men have also been traditionally inept at talking about and working on their relationships with women. It is well known that most men have a "difficulty in expressing emotions." What we say to women is that these traits are cultural problems and learning problems. A number of women have provided the emotion and sensitivity in the relationship, with the men adding rationality and logic. Between the two they try to form a "complete person." This can—temporarily—provide the right fit, but it robs each of developing a well-rounded experience of life. The woman, who gives up her competency in the world of business, economics, academia, or other ways, diminishes herself by living as an infant, helpless and afraid. The man who expresses disdain for emotion with an exaggerated allegiance to intellect and cool objectivity misses out on the depth of feeling, the experience of real contact with other people, and a core sense of the value of his existence. No one gains, and everybody gives up too much self with such ground rules.

While it is true that most men have some incompetence in the expression of feelings or in understanding the emotions behind relationships, it is not true that they cannot do something about these incompetencies. But they will not change if women "take charge" of the category of feelings, nor will they work on the relationships unless women "demand" that they do. Men have to decide to do this on their own.

One of the reasons that most men are terrified to express their feelings is that what they have mostly seen modeled in the arena of feelings is anger and violence and very little else. They don't know much about other emotions such as fear, grief or sadness; better said, they know on a very deep level, way down, a great deal about these feelings, but they have "nowhere to go with them." They have not learned from fathers or other men a way of feeling and talking about feelings that fits their own body. They have not been given permission to express a full range of emotions, nor been expected to develop their thinking about their own body sensations or states of feeling. Awareness about the body and identification of feeling has been trained to be "turned off."

For men, these are things you have to learn from one another. There are a number of excellent ways to learn how to express your feelings in a masculine way. They include working on reconciliation with your father; developing greater intimacy in your male and female friendships; joining therapy or support groups; and serving or dedicating your time to younger men or to boys, either to your own son and his life, or in organizations such as Big Brothers, Scouting, or other community or church-related groups.

Women will likely find it helpful in their relationships with men to stop accepting the unequal burden of expressing all the feelings. Women should avoid the pitfalls of expressing and acting out feelings for the man. They should not be the ones who do all the feeling and talking in the relationship. However, they should remember that roles aren't going to change by Sunday.

One concrete way for women to do this is to refuse to accept the assertion by males that feelings are not important. Second, they should develop their own thinking and problem-solving strategies. That is, they should assess and make plans of their own, based on their own judgment, and not always go to "him" and ask what to do. Let's face it, many women often don't like the way a man solves problems anyway!

In another sphere, a woman might stop running interference by refusing to be the one to call his parents and make arrangements for holidays or get-togethers. Another suggestion is for her to refuse to talk with his parents about "his problems" or "his issues." A woman needs to step out of the man's initiating with his parents and particularly with his own father. She can recommend, but not demand, that he do the connecting with them. Remember, it's his choice, his family, his life.

Simultaneously, it is essential for women to understand more fully their own views about men. They need to reflect on their experience with men, including male friends, coworkers, but especially father. They need to assess whether their experiences and views encourage greater depth in relationships with men or discourage it. If a woman has not resolved (or is working on resolving) her feelings toward her father, it is unlikely she will be able to resolve those feelings with her husband. She too should consider the importance of resolving leftover issues with her own father as part of a connection with the men of her generation, and the future generation she may produce.

We would ask, do you idealize your father? Hate him? How do you compare your lover or husband with your father or brothers, and how does that comparison influence your current relationship? Are there any patterns in your relationships with men that seem similar to your relationship with your father or brothers? Can other men stand on their own merits or do they always get compared to men you have previously had relationships with, either in your family or previous beaus? Do you want to live in the way that your mother did, or some other way? What is the model of manhood and masculinity in your family of origin? Do you pick someone who batters or drinks or rages or is irresponsible? Or someone who can boss around, control, and degrade? A close and careful perusal of these past relationships will give you a chance to scrutinize your current relationships.

Here is a summary of our suggestions to men in simple terms.

1. Stop expecting women to embody your feelings. You have the responsibility for discovering, identifying, and expressing your own feelings in a way that is your own and that can help you discover your mature manhood.
2. Stop expecting women to give you an understanding of what it means to be a man; that cannot come from her. Find that understanding of masculinity from other men, from your own father, from friends, or in therapy with a male therapist.
3. Get competent at home and do your share of housework and childrearing. Get involved! It will have good results on your kids, on you, and on your marriage.
4. Work on a reconciliation with your father.

Tough work, but worth it.

Chapter 10

A Teacher Who Is Excellent

The Role of the Mentor

The mentor is a natural extension of the father in the world outside the home. Often he is the same age as the father, has considerable experience, and has acquired a certain level of wisdom, knowledge, and skill. He has learned many things through life experience in an area that the young man holds dear. He can offer many of the same things a father can, and may evoke in the young man similar feelings of reverence and esteem. However, there are critical differences in the two relationships.

A mentor can (though he does not always) interact with his apprentice without the same emotional intensity that fathers have with their sons. He is able to see the young man more clearly without the interference of emotional ties—the family history—that oftentimes bind and restrict meaningful interaction. The mentor is able to appreciate the skills, differences, and untapped potential and creativity of an apprentice without the blood bond contaminating his vision.

A mentor is able to support his apprentice in new and valuable ways, ways perhaps distinct from a father. This is especially true for an artistic or "unusual" young man whose father may see him as a "bum." The mentor, without the incredible emotional tugs, is able to see past the rebellion, the stubbornness, beyond anger and disappointment; he can see these characteristics as the "usual nonsense" of creativity and help the young man develop beyond these traits into productive use of his talent.

The mentor's job has not often been treated in detail. Our hope is to formulate some "job descriptions" for the mentor, some "how-tos" for him; and to make suggestions to young men on how to choose and use a mentor—the practical steps in finding one, and the best attitude and approach for getting the most out of the relationship.

The job of the mentor is that of a second father, with some aspects of a spiritual director. His job is to teach the young man how to connect with the world and forge a connection between his talents and the world he lives in. The spiritual director helps the young man develop his inner world. The mentor helps him take these discoveries and move them into real life and make a "success" of them. If the mentor can work in both ways—with inner and outer worlds—he will be a great treasure for his apprentice. If he really is only best in one of the two areas, he should encourage his apprentice to find someone else to tackle the other work. Both mentor and spiritual director should be able to communicate a kind of detachment from life's ups and downs and a reliance upon internal strengths and faith and confidence in oneself. He should teach how to see beyond "details" such as specific job promotions, worries about the immediate success of one's current projects, criticism from superiors, and the like.

The job of the mentor is implicit in the word *mentor*, which comes from Latin *mentus* and *minotor*. The original meanings of these words are "advising, warning, and admonishing." These functions, plus "recognizing" and "appreciating," add up to a good description of the role of the mentor.

In interviews about their careers, golf professionals such as Jack Nicklaus, Tom Watson, and Ben Crenshaw all confess to the importance of a mentor for their success. Their mentors taught them skills and corrected bad habits, but beyond that, they taught a positive attitude toward winning and losing, the value of patience and dedication, and the importance of integrity and fairness. Each of these sports heroes views his mentor with fondness and respect. Each mentor appreciated the worth of his apprentice, monitored his progress, and admonished him to be forthright and to gain his highest level of ability.

The first job of the mentor is to advise his apprentice. This is different from a father's advice in the sense that the apprentice is seen as an adult striving to become a colleague in the field—unless the father is in the same field of endeavor, in which case, it is his job to appreciate his son as a colleague also, over time.

To advise means to take a position, not to overwhelm with one's opinion. The mentor should use expressions such as "this seems to me," and "this seems to be true." He should ideally suggest possibilities, not require adherence to his point of view (some cranky old—and young—men see their way as the right and only way). He ought to model three important attributes: autonomy, potency, and modesty. First, the mentor models autonomy by taking a particular position that he strongly believes in, and lives by.

Interestingly, a fourteen-year-old boy, Brett, whom I worked with, had an understanding he communicated about "winners" and "losers." He said that the difference was that "a winner thinks for himself" and a "loser lets MTV think for him." My young sage succinctly reminded me that the mentor's job is to help the apprentice learn the process of becoming a "winner," an autonomous man, who can think and make decisions or actions based on carefully considered values and beliefs.

The mentor embodies modesty by realizing his own limits and recognizing that he cannot be all things for the apprentice. He models how to live through the difficulties and disappointments of the world, and that both gains and losses are to be expected, that they come and go. He should strive to embody a combination of modesty and potency. By potency we mean the ability to hold and act on autonomous beliefs, even when they are unpopular or contrary to current wisdom.

A good example of the mentor who models the combination of modesty and potency is demonstrated in the movie *Bull Durham*. The new, puffed up, self-aggrandizing pitcher is advised by the old battle-scarred catcher to "work with him" in order to be an effective pitcher, to work on his control. The young man is a powerful and tremendous hurler, but has not learned how to use "finesse" or to manage his power, how to combine speed and control, nor how to choose the right pitch in the right circumstances. The catcher (mentor) has acquired a certain modesty that comes with knowing the game, with having been around the game long enough to know that pure speed is not enough. He has a sense of "continuity" and wisdom that has kept him in the sport he loves, doing the work he loves, though his own talent is rather limited. He knows these "young studs" and their style. He is able to let the new pitcher muddle around and make a lot of errors. He knows that his advice will only be taken when the pitcher has been embarrassed and has failed at his all-out approach to pitching. What began as a territorial battle between catcher and raw recruit progresses to the point where the apprentice integrates his lesson well enough to move on to "the show," to the major leagues.

A second quality of the mentor is to "warn" his apprentice—to alert him to dangers, and even occasionally to startle him. In the movie *Bull Durham,* when the young pitcher refuses to take the advice of the veteran, the catcher gives him the sign for a pitch which the batter slugs out of the park. The warning was, "You have to use me in order to make it; if you don't, then I am going to let you screw up." The mentor demands an alertness, a firm connection with the realities of the world around him. He confronts the brashness and cockiness of his apprentice. The good mentor will confront not out of anger but of a sort of amusement or detachment. Again, this is often more easily accomplished by a mentor than by a father. The mentor throws back his arms, kicks his feet up on the desk, looks his apprentice square in the eye and says, "If you do that you are going to screw up."

The apprentice may take the warning from the mentor in a way he would not from his father. They may even be saying the same things. However, the father is seen as being "preachy and controlling," whereas the mentor is being "frank, hard-nosed, and informative."

Mentoring is not without some pitfalls. One of the difficulties for many young men who seek the help of a mentor is that they have not reconciled or resolved their relationship with their own father, and have "burrs in their ass." When they go to an advisor or mentor, they often idealize him beyond his ability, or alternately attempt to run him down, and debase him.

When the apprentice idealizes his mentor, he accords him a level of perfection, hanging on his every word or idea.

He fails to notice imperfections and sometimes blindly follows the mentor without examining his motives or fantasies. Joseph is a young man who had incredible motivation to "make it big" in the investment world. He worked very hard to get the attention of Earl, a well-known kingpin of investments in the Midwest. Earl got Joseph to invest money that he had inherited from his grandparents in an investment ploy that kept Joseph tied to Earl for five years. Just after Joseph had signed the papers, Earl smiled at him and said, "Boy, I got you by the balls. Never sign anything without having an attorney look at it." The result was that Joseph fell further and further into debt on a bad investment, and was legally committed to it and to working for Earl; and Earl, who had made the deal as a tax write-off for himself, ended up with one more "incredible deal" in his pocket. Joseph had chosen a mentor poorly, led by his own greed and by Earl's reputation. He did not ask himself whether this was a man he really wanted to emulate as a person as well as a "successful investor." It is important to consult your own motives first. On the other hand, an apprentice who maliciously or gratuitously runs down his mentor sabotages his own efforts to be instructed or helped, and gets in his own way by inflating his own image of himself. Either position distorts the beneficial influence a capable mentor can have on the apprentice's life.

Even with these potential hazards, a mentor can certainly operate as a father substitute for sons who have missed that deep connection with a father. The relationship with a mentor can be a very rewarding experience in a young man's life. In fact, it can become as important as a blood relationship, or more so, and leave an impression that lasts a lifetime. Not only does the mentor help his pupil find himself in the world, but he also affirms him and substantiates his worth.

What has your experience been like as a mentor or as an apprentice to someone else? The following questions will help you assess your experience.

- Have you had a mentor, or been a mentor to someone else? If so, how did you begin to work together? What held your relationship together? What were some benefits or problems that arose in your work together?
- What influences have mentors been on your decisions in life, your education, career, relationships, religious, sexual, and free-time activity choices?
- In what ways do you see yourself having influenced younger men or boys? Is this the influence you hope to have? If not, what would you change about it?
- What would your father say about the mentors you have worked with? Would he support your choices? What would he think of them personally, in terms of their character? What would be your mentor's opinion of your father? How do the answers to these questions affect you? What responses do you have?
- If you have not had a mentor or been a mentor for someone else, how do you explain this situation? What might you want from a mentor, or why might you want to provide guidance for another man?
- In any of the following situations, where were your most positive and most negative experiences of mentoring:

  sports, either as participant or coach
  scouting or summer camp
  academics
  work
  apprenticeship in a skill
  hobbies

In his practice, Steve Sirridge has consulted with a young medical resident in the last year and found that the resident looks to him for guidance both in his career (especially with patient relations) and in his relationships with women. The resident's own father will not talk with him about anything personal or emotional, and he has the opportunity to work on these issues with Steve. He talks about his insecurities, fears, triumphs, mistakes, and disappointments, as well as the joy of learning in his career. Steve finds the mentor's job rewarding. He sees himself as giving this resident an opportunity to use his abilities—which are considerable—to develop as a doctor and to build more of a sense of self.

How can a man find and use a mentor? First, he must be willing to ask for help. This is a difficult thing for many men to do, but absolutely necessary if they are going to develop their full potential in their lives. You must be willing to ask for help and then be willing to use it: to follow the guidelines of the mentor, to subordinate yourself to his judgment, and to be open to someone more experienced than you are.

The mentor ends up with an awesome responsibility in the bargain. But he must realize that he too is serving something greater than himself. This something goes by many names—psyche, God, the higher self—but essentially means that he is serving something beyond his own ego and that he, too, has much to learn.

A Jungian analyst, Arwind Vasavada, wrote a beautiful article called "Fee-less Practice and Soul Work." In this article, he discusses his own life, about moving from India to the United States as an "established older man." In India he had lived on a fixed salary at a university and had just made ends meet. In the United States he found that he could make a good deal of money as an analyst and could be quite successful. However, after a time, he found that he felt a certain sense of malaise about his practice. He went to visit his guru in India, the "blind saint." This saint admonished him to remember the reasons or the values which he had pursued when he first went into the practice of analysis—to serve the psyche and to serve other human beings. Somewhere in his work, Vasavada had lost sight of that primary goal or reason, and the guru served as a "monitor." Vasavada had been lured by money for the first time in his life and had begun to lose his core reasons for practicing. His guru told him he should practice without a set fee, in other words, he should do his work and tell his patients to pay what they could.

He put the guru's suggestions into effect, but found himself in a kind of chaos. Some people would pay a few dollars, or not at all, and some would pay the "going rate" for analysis. There was a broad variation in the amount of money that he would get at any given time, and it was difficult work. But he found that he was regaining appreciation for his original decision to practice therapy. He also found after a number of years that if he averaged his income and patient load over time, he came out with a fairly consistent and dependable income over the long term.

Part of the job of the mentor is to point out the evenness of life, to help the apprentice see beyond the ups and downs of daily living. Another duty is to remind the apprentice, even to admonish him, of his commitment and original decisions to do the work he is doing. This path is easy to lose in the chaos and stress most of us encounter every day. The mentor steers his apprentice back to his original reasons which brought him to a master: to seek the core meaning and value of his life within the world.

When the mentor sees his apprentice following a route which he thinks is a dead end (thought he may ultimately be wrong in this opinion), it is his job to tell the apprentice so and suggest other options, other possibilities, and alternate ways of proceeding. He steers the apprentice in ways he thinks are most profitable for him.

Another job of the mentor is to assign tasks, trials, and problems to the apprentice. In the university it is fairly easy to see how this is achieved, because the mentor assigns his advisee specific problems to solve (a thesis, research project, or the like). In other work it may be harder to specify, but the principle is the same—to assign activity and thinking exercises which help the apprentice learn the complexities of the world.

An enjoyable illustration of this process can be seen in the *Karate Kid* movies. A young boy wants to learn to be a karate expert and goes to a master. The master assigns tasks which seem to be irrelevant (at first) to learning karate, such as waxing a car or sanding wood. It is only after the kid has mastered these movements and then is shown how to apply them to self-defense that he is able to see the relevance of the practice. Before that he had little idea of how waxing a car would help him toward becoming a martial arts expert. He eventually accomplishes his goal, in part because of his willingness to submit to the master's directives, and in part due to his stubborn attention to learning the tasks assigned to him, regardless of whether he understands their purpose or not.

This kind of selflessness on the part of an apprentice and control on the part of the master is all well and good in the hands of a compassionate master. But some sadistic mentor could have his apprentice do useless, meaningless things that humiliate him and degrade him to no good end For this reason, we advise choosing a mentor with care and attention. Our advice in the "More Resources" Chapter at the end of the book on "choosing a therapist" is directly applicable to the process of choosing a mentor.

In this light, the final job of the mentor, and perhaps his most important job, is to recognize and appreciate his apprentice, and to have compassion for him. He attempts to honestly recognize the worth, the innate value, as well as the skills and competence of the younger man. This can be difficult, because it may require the mentor to stifle his own desire to compete with the apprentice. What a mentor often finds is that an apprentice chose him in order to eventually surpass him. It is hard to be graceful with someone who plans to far surpass your achievements, but that is the mentor's job: grace and tolerance. Grace, in this sense, means remembering his own history of dreams, efforts, accomplishments, and failures. One day the apprentice may be expressing his admiration and praise for the mentor, through his growing and developing with the mentor's monitoring. A mentor's reward is the achievement of his apprentice; he may never express his appreciation outright.

Just as the father has a difficult time accepting his own failures, the mentor will find himself discovering his own limits. Apprentices will come who have far greater innate talents than his own. The apprentice may be the one who moves on to the major leagues, develops a new medical approach, becomes the successful professional musician, or creates a lucrative business; any of these may have been the mentor's unrealized goal for himself.

What role should a father play in this process, and how can he be helpful to his son as he moves into the world on his own? A part of the job of the father is to prepare his son to find a mentor; here are three ways this can be accomplished.

1. The father must reconcile issues with his own father,

so he isn't "stuck" being a father and trying to compensate for his own personal lacks, by "overdoing" with his son, making up for what he didn't get. He must work on himself, so he isn't depending on the son for the realization of his own goals, ambitions, or hopes in life. This helps him let go of his son, and enables the son to feel freed from having to live for his father's sake.

2. He can encourage his son to find out what will be his field of interest, and then encourage him to find mentors. He can share his perceptions of what the son might be "good at," and try to help the son see himself and his talents realistically, viewing his strengths and weaknesses. And, most significant, if the son is choosing areas of interest which the father does not know well, the father must have the courage and strength to admit his ignorance openly and to suggest, encourage, and support the son's getting help from someone who knows that area of interest well.

The two worst things a father can say to his son in this area of life are, "you are worthless and will never amount to anything," and "you can do anything you want." Neither statement helps the son get a good start in life, with a realistic appraisal of his talents and his direction. Interestingly, both statements can have the effect of a condemnation. Sometimes, the second one ("you can do anything") is even perceived as a "worse" curse. Some men get over the idea that they will "never amount to anything" by outright rejection of the father's statement as nothing more than hostility, drunkenness, or ignorance, and then moving on into life, through many of them will overwork themselves to "try to prove him wrong."

But the notion that "you can do anything" is sometimes a harder curse to shake. If a young man is given this message, he might believe that anything he does is not good enough since, if he can do anything, he ought to be always doing something even better than what he is currently doing. Men who are trying to live up to this view of themselves tend to work themselves to death.

An alternative is for the father to help his son get a realistic understanding of his strengths and weaknesses. The father may have some way of assessing these, given his own experience in life. He can encourage his son to get other help as well, such as talking to school counselors, to people in the lines of endeavor the son shows interest in, and by discussing as thoroughly as possible with the son what he himself sees as his capabilities. This is good and useful guidance. The point is to help the son get a clear sense of what he does well, and how to develop these talents. The choice of whether he follows the guidance is, of course, ultimately up to the son. But whatever he chooses as his path in life, once he has chosen, it then becomes the father's job to do his best to understand and support his son's choices wherever possible.

3. Finally, the father's job is to let go of his son and let him grow up in his own way, when the son shows readiness to choose his own guidance and tutelage from other people. His son may still ask him for guidance, but if he is already grown and doesn't ask, the father must not interfere; rather, the father's job is to remain emotionally connected and interested in his son. In time, they may develop a friendship as men together in the world.

A conscientious mentor will realize the honor—and sometimes, burden—he has been given by having been chosen by his apprentice. He is a "second father" and, as such, can have a deep influence on his apprentice. He can communicate to his apprentice ways to approach work, views on life and its meaning, and the dangers and rewards of effort. He embodies and older man who has survived the doubts, hesitations, and anxieties of the apprentice. He has the opportunity to impart whatever wisdom and hope he has to the young man who has chosen him for a guide.

Chapter 11

Inner Reconciliation of Father and Son

Earlier we discussed the things that the father can do to have an impact on raising his son from infancy through childhood. Now we are going to focus on the adult male, both as father and as son. You doubtless have found aspects of your relationship with your father that remain unattended to. You may feel some nagging sense of incompleteness or dissatisfaction with your relationship. So let's look at how reconciliation between the father and the son can be important, useful, even necessary. We will be talking here about "inner reconciliation," that is, the reconciliation within yourself, between your own internal Father and your internal Son.

Men who have not experienced a reconciliation with their father don't seem to achieve the kind of confidence, self-possession, authority, determination, or decisiveness they might be capable of. They betray a kind of floundering in relationships and work, a vulnerability to addictions, and an inability to be playful. With many men there is a prevailing or nagging sense that relationships with other men and women are unsatisfactory. One of the ways we see this manifested is the way many men stay angry throughout their lives. In the cases of such men, reconciliation between father and son has not taken place literally, on the outside, nor within themselves, in their inner world.

How can you experience reconciliation with your father within yourself? What can that mean? Let us introduce two terms. There is a father principle, which we call "authority," and a son principle, which we call "discipleship." Every person, male or female, operates under the influence of these principles as part of the makeup of the psyche.

What we mean by the father within is represented by authority—the archetypal or unconscious father. This authority is that sense of fathering we can identify with in the qualities of confidence, determination, self-possession, decisiveness, and calm power.

The son, the unconscious son, is represented by the principle of discipleship, which includes qualities of vulnerability and hopefulness. These in turn are manifested in the traditional imagery of the disciple—one who comes to the authority to learn, grow, develop, and change, perhaps to challenge and question.

What we see in a number of men is a conflict or battle between authority and discipleship as well as a tendency to get stuck in one pole or the other. One who gets stuck in the pole of authority becomes authoritarian, overbearing, controlling, dominant—what the feminists have identified in their writings on the patriarch. The negative side of the patriarch is manifested by a subordinating, enslaving attitude of authority, an attitude which seems to say, "the world is inferior to me." His is not a real sense of authority. His is an attempt to steal power from others, rather than having come into his own power. The attempt to dominate others is a form of addiction which requires ever-increasing control over the subordination of others. It results in greater and greater anxiety, paranoia, and terror, because it can topple and disintegrate at any moment, when one shows weakness or any normal human sensitivity. To be stuck in the pole of authority is a death sentence, because you become obsessed with power, fear that you will lose your control, and are suspicious of other people.

Many men swing strongly to the side of discipleship. This is the kind of man we see wandering around looking for something to happen. He is constantly searching for something to make his life right, to "turn it around," to give meaning to his life. This something can take the form of food, sports, sex, drugs. He hopes it will confer a sense of authority on him. This kind of discipleship is exemplified by the son who finds himself leaving home, to find something which will make life exciting, good, and meaningful. A couple of months later he inevitably returns home, penniless, in debt, exhausted, but perhaps with some interesting "treasures" he has found in his travels. These treasures may indeed be valuable. They may be the experience of having encountered cultures different from his, rare or unusual items found in remote places (such as handmade art objects), friendships with people from around the world, or self-knowledge in one form or another.

We are reminded of the adventures of Indiana Jones, who spends his life in search of ancient treasure and discovering the secrets of old civilizations. "Indy" embodies the brash young hero, open to adventure and challenge, but also an authority in his field. Yet, he is driven by his hunger for adventure from one challenge to another; he is restless, unsettled, and dissatisfied despite all his accomplishments. It is in the final episode of the movie series, *The Search for the Grail,* that we find out about his competition with his father and his struggle to be recognized by him. By the end of the movie, the two seemed to have resolved conflicts between them, and each man seems more settled and satisfied with himself in his sense of his own authority and competence.

Both the sense of authority and the sense of discipleship have tremendous value in themselves but much more when they are joined and integrated. They hold much more potential when they are reconciled. The quality of authority is good in its effectiveness. It's imbued with a certain solidity and power. Discipleship encompasses other qualities, such as openness, adaptability, and excitement. An important step in the reconciliation of father and son is the potent integration which comes from the befriending of authority and discipleship. This is the place where determination and solidity meet vulnerability and hope.

Men often move from one pole to the other, or find themselves stuck at one pole. Some men are in the position of dominance and control—or try to be—all the time. Then there is another group who find themselves continually in the position of seeking some kind of definition for themselves. Men who stay in this position of discipleship never experience the authority to imbue themselves with a sense of confidence. They are always in flux, always searching, always looking for someone to tell them how to "do it better." They are in search of one mentor after another, or one guru after another. Men caught in the self-imposed trap of authority, of having to be in the position of dominance, lose sight of the fact that for everyone who is an authority in one setting, there is always someone who supercedes them in another. The father without the influence of the son rigidifies an attitude. He says, don't do it that way, do it this way, learn from my experience. It is his overidentification with authority that is attempting to dictate to others how to feel, think, and act.

A richly informed, powerful position of self-confidence comes from the ability to move from the quality of authority (the father) to the disciple (the son) and to know both sides of oneself in whatever one encounters. This means commanding authority where it is possible and appropriate and also experiencing discipleship where that is right and necessary.

Here is an exercise in visualization* which uses imagination to help you identify the characteristics of your own inner authority and inner disciple. This exercise can be done in a group or with two people.

Begin by finding a quiet place to lie down or sit to release all the tension in your body. Find a place where you can stretch out and will not be bothered. Let the chair or floor support you. Take several deep breaths. As you inhale, imagine that you are inhaling peaceful, calm energy. As you exhale, let out tension and breathe into areas of tightness that you have in your body. With each exhalation, allow yourself to carry the oxygen more and more deeply into your body. Imagine that it is going into every cell of your body. Again, as you exhale, imagine that you are sending away nervousness, tightness, difficulties that you have experienced.

Pay attention to each part of your body to see that you are resting and letting go of tension throughout your body. Tense for a moment each place that feels tight, then let it relax, and feel supported by the surfaces you are resting on. Now, begin by imagining that you are lying outdoors, in a place that appeals to you, where you have not been before. Imagine that it is a bright, softly lighted day. The weather is mild. Imagine that you are at peace with yourself as you begin this journey. Imagine that you can feel the breeze

*Contributed by Joel Vogt, a counselor and art therapist.

moving over you; experience the smells and the colors that are around you.

Look in each direction and see what the landscape holds. Trees? Grass? Are there signs of wildlife? Now, as you slowly begin to look in the distance, you will see a path. It is on this path that you must walk.

When you are ready, stand up in your imagination and begin your journey. Start by looking at the path to see what it looks like. Is it rocky, is it smooth, is it straight? Is it narrow or wide? This perhaps is symbolic of the kind of path which will lead you to your inner guide.

Follow along this path and continue walking. Leave your original position and be aware of this path taking you further and further into a forest. After you are deep in the forest, you will discover that this path leads upward. Slowly but surely you begin to ascend.

After traveling a long time, you begin to rise above the trees. By this time it is approaching darkness. As you reach the summit, the moon is very bright. You can see very far. You can see a fire. This fire provides light and also hope.

As you walk closer to the fire, you notice what is nearby, rocks, shadowy trees. What else do you see? As you approach, be aware of someone sitting beside the fire. He is waiting for you. Across the fire, look into his eyes. Be aware of his acceptance of you and of any other messages his expression communicates to you. Be aware also of your own acceptance or rejection of his appraisal of you.

Experience now as you study him, his attitude toward you. Notice the power and strength he has, his manner of showing his self-assurance and confidence, his way of holding himself, how he makes contact with you. Again assess your ability to accept the gift of his acceptance of you, and the comfort that he has in reaching out to you. His wisdom is being offered to you. At this moment, he is willing and ready to give you a token of his confidence in you.

He is reaching toward you to hand you something. Reach out to accept it. After he has handed you this object, look at it carefully. Take it in your hands and hold it, examine it. Be aware too of any uncertainties you have, of your hesitations, of limitations that you feel. Allow yourself to know that those exist and that you can accept them.

And, after you are finished with this meeting, move back into your own space for just a moment, breaking contact with your guide. When you look back up, he will not be there.

If you are ready for this next step, you will take the risk to move into his space. Get up and go to the position he was sitting in before. Imagine yourself as the guide. Carry yourself the way he was carrying himself. Experience the same sense of confidence. Experience the sense of strength and assuredness of having authority and wisdom.

Remember, it is your right to take this position. As you sit experiencing yourself as the guide, look out over the fire again. See yourself as you were a few moments ago, across the fire. See a man who has not fully taken up his own confidence, that was a disciple. See a man who has not found his own authority yet, his own wisdom.

He is a seeker of wisdom. Look at that man carefully. That man was you. See yourself through the eyes of wisdom. What can you find out about yourself from this position? What can you know about yourself?

Now move back into the position of the seeker or student yourself. See yourself as the disciple. How would you like to see yourself differently? What path would you take that is different from the one you are currently on?

After you have thought about all these things, decide

how you would like to return to the position from which you began this journey, what new awarenesses and strengths you will take back. When you go, remember to take with you the keepsake that was given to you. After you have decided how to get back, return to where you began.

After you have done this exercise, you may want to do a few things to help consolidate what you have experienced or learned. Here are some suggestions for how to do this:

1. You may wish to make a piece of art which is a representation of the token you received from the wise man.
2. Write down in a journal what you experienced, where you went, what you saw, what you learned.
3. Decide what other journeys you would like to go on from the position from which you began.
4. List the blocks or limitations you feel you have and what would help you to deal with them.
5. Remember what your path in the guided image was like, and mentally check whether the path you have taken in life is similar to the imaginary path and if that is how you wish it to be. If it is different, what would you like to incorporate into your daily life? What are the qualities of the path in your exercise, and how could you use these characteristics to enrich your life?

One example of the combination of authority and discipleship is demonstrated by Carl Jung in his autobiography. Late in life, after having analyzed tens of thousands of dreams, Jung—who is certainly one of our greatest authorities on dreams—writes that the proper way to approach a dream is to assume first of all, "I don't understand this dream. I don't know what this dream means." This prepares one for an attitude of learning from the context and information in a dream. There is the quality of discipleship. But he also said that in order to understand the dream, one must know a lot about culture, literature, mythology, religion, the dreamer's personal background, and have some clinical training. This is a good example of the fruitful combination of authority and discipleship.

Another example comes from the Zen Buddhism tradition. The title of one of D. T. Suzuki's books is *Zen Mind, Beginner's Mind.* One Zen master is quoted as saying that the proper mind is the beginner's mind. And this is from one of the masters. Both the sense of having experience and also of being awake to new possibilities are combined in this attitude.

A reconciliation between authority and discipleship is the masculine attitude that the great Greek folk hero Odysseus personifies as he wanders the seas. He is a king and he is also an adventurer. As a king in his own land, in Ithaca, he has the power of the father, and is the authority figure there. When he is adventuring in new lands, he is not a king, but rather a discoverer exploring new lands. So on the one hand he is the one who knows, who has potency, cunning, and strength. On the other hand, he is the one who is vulnerable and exposed to a new world of wonders unfolding at every turn.

As a psychologist, I spend a good deal of my time supervising other people in the practice of psychotherapy. I find myself in the position of directing, and of being the expert and authority. Yet at times I find myself growing weary of that role. There is a part of me—the adventuresome part—longing for new information, for new possibilities. That is the part of me that moves to start learning again from someone else. This keeps a balance between being the patriarch in one setting and a disciple in another. The latter contains an adventuresome spirit in the search for something new. I want to keep possibilities alive and embrace the idea that there is so much I don't know. That is an exciting possibility and should not be seen as a problem.

What we have to remember is that at any moment, whether we are seeing ourselves as the father or as the son, we are always both. So as an adult male we are fathers—whether we have sons or not. We have the potential of being the father, with power, solidity, influence, and the like. But the adult man always carries the flip side of solidity and success, that is, disillusionment, the loss of dreams, and potential. It is inevitable that we carry both the father's strength and his failures.

But we all also share the qualities of the son, the freshness, the vitality, the sense of the infinite, as well as the narcissist desire to be gratified at every instant. He also embodies the dual structure of obedience and rebellion. However, the son also personifies some less exciting elements. He may feel frustrated at not being paid attention to. He may be laughed at, and told he is inadequate because he is too young, too green, too inferior.

A reconciliation of these two means that as a father (both the father within and as a literal father), our biggest job with the son is to learn to accept the son's discipleship. This means accepting and honoring the trust and love that the son wants to give to the father. We can accept that there is a part within ourselves that wants to serve a higher, more developed self within—to serve and obey and challenge the father.

As a son, what we must learn to accept from the father is his authority; we can begin to learn from the father, from his knowledge, from his power and understanding. We should know that we don't have to be alone and face every storm and difficulty without him. Each of us has a place of incompetence and a place of vulnerability and wonder within that wants to be helped by the father.

One of the hardest things for young to middle-aged men to do today is to love their competence, to love their power, to love their knowledge and experience and influence: to love their father. Today's "thirty-something" men seem to present a facade of competence. They are "all work and no play," as a friend of ours, Linda, has said. However, their drive seems to come more from an addictive, restless attitude than from a calm, secure sense of themselves.

Men who grew up in the fifties and sixties learned to hate and mistrust their fathers. The father, with his power and competence, was viewed as evil. The sons despised their fathers, since the sons felt consistently lied to about their country, about politics, about Vietnam. Many of their worst suspicions about the treachery, meaninglessness, and insanity of being in Vietnam turned out to be true. We found out about the abuses perpetrated by older men in South America and Central America, the destruction of people, land, and cultures by our government. We learned about the wholesale destruction and abuse of our natural resources sanctioned by our government. How could this group then trust older men?

Competence, authority, and masculinity certainly were not to be trusted or loved; the father perpetrated evil. The jury has returned on this one, and to some degree it is true. But that has left this generation with an enormous sense of loss—of masculinity, fatherhood, confidence, and determination.

One of the things about reconciliation is to be reconciled

to the mystery of our own darkness; to be reconciled to the mystery of that part of ourselves which we have rejected or scorned or thrown away as bad or evil. What we know from the world's mythology, from all the cosmologies of the world's religions and from our own experience, is that light comes out of the darkness. Possibilities of new development arise from the darkest and most remote places. In many folktales—those mirrors of our unconscious—we often find that the stupidest, youngest son is always the one who comes up with the answer to the king's riddle. The place in the cosmos that is the darkest and most remote is where the light comes from. God's light shines in the darkness—that is where it shines, and it is up to us to recognize it.

These places of darkness in men, these wounds, are exactly the places of pain from which our greatest strength will arise. The lesions are the places of healing. Within the Christian story, Jesus came to Thomas and showed him his wound. When Thomas saw and felt the wound of Jesus, he could move into his discipleship with resolution. When we look into our lesions, we will most often see a father and a son turned away from each other and longing to know each other. The immediateness of experiencing the wounds of the son and the father is the place where the transformation or development can come from.

Jesus says, "I and the Father are one." In addition to theological meanings we might take from Jesus's statement, another interpretation is that he had combined or reconciled the qualities of son and father within himself. He owned his authority and his competence and power to know his own knowledge and the knowledge of the patriarchs before him; but he had also submitted himself and made himself vulnerable and open to discovering and being humiliated. He did not lose his sense of authority. He kept both authority and vulnerability to the end. I think that is a paramount lesson of the crucifixion: I and the father are one—authority and discipleship are joined.

The time preceding his crucifixion is his darkest hour, where he plunges into his own despair. Even on the cross he says, "Father, Father, why have you forsaken me?" This is exactly the place where men find themselves today, asking this question. What Jesus found in his own transcendence is that he was not forsaken. This is where many men enter into their own woundedness. They suddenly can't find their authority. They look around, but it is not there; the father is missing. Where did it go? In a number of cases it never was there in the first place. They were faking it.

This lack of connection with the internal father when it is needed most is a theme we explored in earlier chapters. This connection is integral to a real sense of confidence, balance, and power. Discipleship as the only routine has run its course. The adult is too old for that and cannot pull off the child prodigy routine anymore; cuteness, silliness, and talent no longer are enough. Even women don't find him cute anymore. Conversely, when the sole qualities of an adult male authority go bankrupt, there is no longer anything inside to draw on: one has become dried out. Inside, you know that your braggadocio is only a thin crust; there is nothing under it. If someone leans on it, you believe you'll crumble. You embody no well to draw on, no adventure, no sense of newness or possibility.

The internal reconciliation of father and son is a totality of some kind. Each requires the other. Together they lead to the development of our capacity for honor, consciousness, pleasure, enjoyment, meaning, and self-understanding.

To apply these principles to yourself, you might want to make an inventory of your own resources. What is your sense of your authority? Where do you feel self-confident, assured, potent? In what areas of life—work, relationships, sports, artistic talent, mechanical ability, and the like—do you sense that you have authority? These are the areas of your self-fathering, the areas where your own internal father is strong.

Where do you feel curious and drawn to explore? Where do you feel weak, longing for the power of some order and knowledge? Where do you find yourself wanting guidance, help, understanding? In what ways do you wish to serve something or someone higher than you—a cause, a person, an idea? In which ways do you express your belief, your devotion, your willingness to learn and develop? These are the areas of your sonship.

Inner reconciliation is an integration of your own internal father and son, the father embodying authority and the son discipleship. Even as a man moves toward a greater sense of inner authority and self-possession, he must also retain the exuberance to learn and grow, and the brashness to search after and challenge himself and others. A richly informed position of self-confidence comes from the capacity to know both sides of oneself in whatever one encounters. To know this, and to act on this, will sustain a man through the process of self-discovery and self-mastery.

Chapter 12

Reconciliation of Father and Son

The topic of reconciliation needs to be addressed from several vantage points. One is from the adult son's side, from a man thirty to forty-five years of age or so, who has a dawning recognition that there has been and continues to be something significant missing in his relationship with his father. Also, we need to consider the vantage point of the older father, who may be moving toward or has already reached retirement age, and observes his own son growing older, taking on the role of a father. He himself may view his role as somewhat disengaged or distant from his son, and is wishing at this point to form a close connection with him.

First, let's consider adult sons who are perceptive enough to recognize that a gap exists between yourself and your father. You have the responsibility of initiating contact. It is not enough to recognize significant distance or estrangement or some kind of benevolent neutrality between the two of you. It also won't help for you to be angry and resentful of the situation and sit on it by rationalizing that, "It's dad's responsibility to do something about this." If you take this obstinate stance, you are perpetuating the fantasy that you are still a little boy, without the power to make things happen. You are acting as if you're a young boy waiting for his father to direct, confront, and guide. The reality is different, because now you are grown and a man in your own right, with the ability to make choices and act in a more direct and responsible manner. With recognition of the problem also comes the responsibility to initiate a reconciliation.

How do you move across this gulf, this chasm which is now thirty, forty, even fifty years old? Do you just send a long letter or knock on dad's door and say, "Let's talk about our relationship?" Probably not. Before letters are sent, and meetings demanded or arranged, there is internal work that you as a son need to do in preparation for this important step. There is a lot of thinking and feeling work you should do in advance. This includes bringing internal feelings to the surface and making them concrete, making them come alive. By giving internal feelings external shape, as through art, the inner experience becomes more real, approachable, understandable. For each person this can take a little different form. One man might write in a journal, another do a piece of art, a third may find and sing or play a song or even write a song that really expresses how the relationship with his father feels inside. Another, with skills as a carpenter, might make a box in which to put something symbolic that represents his feelings. Even if you never have done art, you might try just getting your feelings out with paper and magic markers or paint. Making a finished art product is not the point, so don't worry about what it looks like. The point is just to express something inside of you. Making art or some kind of creative product can make things plainer, more concrete. It makes something that you can put your hands on, touch, see, hear, use your senses to immediately perceive.

You have the responsibility to get off your duff and bring up whatever has lazed and ground around inside, and make it more clear, distinct, and honest. There is a direct level of ownership possible when you see what your feelings have produced on paper, on canvas, in clay; this kind of ownership can get things moving.

This is a way to begin. You owe this to yourself and to your father. By using art materials, spontaneous writing, or other methods, you can begin to say things in a basic, primitive way, a way that is not censored or weighted in favor of what future repercussions and consequences might be forthcoming. An example might be to let yourself express feelings such as anger, fear, sadness, joy, disappointment, hurt, and so on, in full-blown form in the materials. Simple statements such as, "I need my father. I need his guidance and his help; where is he? I need his protection. I hate my father; he was never there. I need him to be proud of me," can be expressed in a variety of ways, and are nearly guaranteed to get things moving in your feelings. These feelings can be written, sculpted, yelled, drawn, or sung.

The more direct and simpler the statement, the better. When succinctness or directness is expressed, this allows you to get in touch with parts of you from your youth that have intense feelings about your father. These feelings may not ultimately be what you talk about with your father; however, you will most likely find it useful to be aware of and express these suppressed needs, before deciding what you are going to do about them. It is vital and necessary to know what impact these unconscious feelings have on you as you plan what you want to be saying to dad and what it is you are hoping will come out of all this.

You can ask yourself, "What is still alive for me from the past, what voices or what experiences are still unresolved from my boyhood? What still calls me back to being a boy, a son, with my father? What did I (do I) want from my father: praise? recognition? physical contact? time? to be taught a skill? to talk with him about things going on inside of me?" Write out bold, swift statements, in clear, concise, and simple language. Later you can remind yourself that any relationship is a complex undertaking and that you may be thinking about him in a certain, fixed way, which may not fit who he is today. The critical father you remember may have mellowed or may be sick and dependent. What you are aware of may be distorted by your perspective from "then" as a child and may not tell the whole picture.

Andy, a man I spoke with recently about reconciliation with his father said, "The only thing I am aware of is my anger and my resentment of my father; that's all. I don't see him ever changing." Andy is aware of only one feeling (anger) and that obscures his awareness of any others (like disappointment), as well as the fact that he cannot see his father as capable of changing. His painful childhood memories shade all of his perceptions and feelings. What I am sure will happen for him is that once he draws these feelings out and experiences them, he will begin to be aware of other feelings or thoughts as well.

Thus, in the process of discovering your feelings about your father, it is valuable to note that that relationship has not occurred within a vacuum. It has occurred against the backdrop of a number of other people within your childhood environment. Explorations therefore need to be made with other members of the family on how they perceived your relationship with your father. A similar procedure to that we have been suggesting can take place in acknowledging and expressing feelings about other people in your life—mother, siblings, grandparents, even close neighbors or others who have played a part in the development and life of your family.

You should write letters, to be held back at first and perhaps sent later. You may write a letter to your mother about your relationship with your father. This will obviously take in part of your relationship with your mother, but the focus is with your father. The same thing can be done with your brother or sister or others—especially if you have brothers. Write to your brother or sister about your relationship with your dad. Last—and very important—you might send a letter to your own son or your fantasy son about your relationship with your father. This will carry the impact of how you are relating to your own son, to yourself and to your own father, and will undoubtedly say something very powerful to you about the intergenerational community of men represented in your family.

First, you write, draw, sculpt, make in some concrete form what it is you feel, fantasize, and think inside. Then it is time to make an important decision—whether you are willing to take the risk to enlarge the context—to "take it home." Are you willing to let someone read or see or hear about what you have been doing (not yet the person or persons to whom the material is directed.) For example, you can show a letter meant for your father, mother, or sibling, about your relationship with your father, to a spouse, a close male friend, an uncle, or a therapist. Then you can deal with their responses or reactions, and your own feelings. Some of these people may be important in the sense that what has always perhaps been a secret within you about how you feel about somebody important can be drawn out and shared with others. You can share something very important and very personal with someone else. If that reader is a male, this can be a very powerful and healing experience in itself.

This may or may not be followed by an actual letter sent, a series of face-to-face meetings, or the like. It is logical for that to occur, but it may not happen. You may go on to form closer ties with your father, but it may never be in the way we have been referring to—a thorough going over the past to resolve old wounds. Rather, there may be a reconciliation which takes place fairly silently, with greater contact between the adult son and his father, but with little discussion of the past. The hope is that increased contact may generalize to more open communication.

Some of you have a father who has died or who is terminally ill—or your father is absolutely out of your reach. This should not be an inhibition to you, partly because the human psyche does not necessarily recognize the ordinary accidents of life—such as death. Relationships in the psyche continue regardless of external events. So a relationship with the dead father, in terms of letters and imagined conversations, or actual conversations—for those who experience such things—can certainly take place. And, of course, in the spirit of broadening the context, you can continue connecting with your father through those who are still alive, through memories, experiences, images, and thoughts about him.

After working through some of these preliminary steps of sorting out your emotional position, needs, and desires in the reconciliation with your father, you may want to carry this to the next level. The next step involves finding a direct relationship with your father. For example, if it is "normal" for you to talk with your mother and father when you call their house, you can ask to speak with your father alone, or call him specifically to talk to him. It is quite ordinary today for sons to talk with mom and dad or just mom on the phone, and not just to father. Talk to him alone and monitor yourself to see what "comes up." Is it frightening, exciting? Do you feel sad, angry? What feelings emerge even as you think of doing this? At family gatherings, especially if the parents live at some distance, conscientiously arrange even a short period of time to be alone with your father. Write to your father occasionally— just to him.

What often happens, because of things we discussed in earlier chapters about the development cycle of boys, is that the young boy develops an ease in conversation, in physical proximity with the mother, and still feels most comfortable with her. The continued link with the mother eclipses his link with his father and keeps him in a secret marriage with mom. This makes it very difficult for the son to talk to her "other husband"—his dad, that stranger. For many men who consider the possibility of a direct link with the father, what comes up is a fear of hurting mom, or consequently being abandoned by her. The son already has one big hole where the father never was, a big bucket of grief, and now he risks being abandoned by the mother and having another empty spot. No way!

One of the ways to help ease this problem is to talk to your mother about your need to have a relationship with your father. Tell her that you don't want to sever your relationship with her, that you love her, and that if she begins to feel hurt, this is the natural grief of separation that mothers usually experience when the natural separation process occurs when little boys are two years old—it just has been delayed about forty years, that's all. She'll live through it. This does not mean that the link you had with your mother until now is wrong—far from it. You had the natural desires for closeness, support, someone to talk to about what you did all day long, whom you met, who won or lost the game, what happened in school—someone with a bodily warmth and love for you and an interest in you. Nothing is wrong with that; your father, if he is like most men in their middle years, just plain was not there providing that kind of bodily, emotional, and intellectual nourishment.

You can respect the history of your relationship with your mother and still want to have something different with her, and to have something different with your father. You can respect your desire to have a relationship with your father without that having to be an attack or insult to your mother. This might sound like pretty basic stuff to some of you, but you would be surprised how many men think that their mother has to be hurt or rejected in order to have a relationship with their father.

Most fathers of sons who are now in the middle years have very little idea or understanding of what their sons are asking when they approach them and say "Let's deepen things between us." They will most likely assume that their son (1) had a big falling out with his wife and wants to move back home, (2) needs money, or (3) is drunk or drugged up or gone mad. Don't be surprised, then, if your father seems bewildered, surprised, or even angry while he looks over at your mother to get her interpretation on "what's wrong with the boy now?" Something important to remember is that there is a loving father deep inside of him somewhere, even if it is under an immense pile of garbage, and even if it never gets brought to the surface before he dies. His bewilderment is cultural, it is not innate. Culturally and in the recent history of the family, the father has not had a place with the children. So it is going to come as a surprise that you ask him to be involved with you—don't you be surprised.

If your father was unavailable to you when you were little, remember that chances are he was doing what he thought was right, and what was defined as the way to be a man and father in his younger years. What was meaningful to him at that time was building a career, carving out a place in the world and a home for his family—this was what the title "Father of the Family" conferred in his day. Raising children was not considered the domain of a proper man. Supporting and sustaining a family meant being out in the work world, not being home with the children. One thing to remember is that nothing will ever be gained by shaming your father, or by attempting to extract an apology for his behavior. Although many young men today feel betrayed by their father's inattention to them or attention to them through criticism, an attack and attempt to shame your father for his errors in the past will only lead to more pain, alienation, and distance between the two of you.

Again, this is why we say that it is essential to do your own personal, inner work, to recognize, understand, and express your angers and resentments in their rawest, most vengeful ways, even in their most archaic and most vicious forms. It is necessary to work through these feelings, thoughts, and fantasies first, before you go to your father. We are not saying, don't be angry or sad or disappointed with your father, don't show him these feelings—to the contrary! What we are saying is that it is useful, meaningful, and effective to sort out your thoughts, feelings, and fantasies, to know more about them, to know more about yourself before you go unleashing them on the world. You will find that the first group of feelings and fantasies—often anger, homicidal rage—is perhaps more of a cover-up for what is deeper—grief, longing, and desire for nearness with your father. You will find all kinds of things you don't know about before you explore inside. It will serve you well to look around inside and find out what is really there.

You—and your father—deserve this kind of preparation. You owe it to yourself and to him to do some inner work before you try to reconnect with him. But why? You might still insist he is an asshole! "He never did anything for me!" This really gives you more reason to look at your own inner reactions, thoughts, and feelings before you talk to him. If you attack him and shame him, how will he respond? Think about it logically. Which do you want more, revenge or a better relationship with him?

If you want to do something for yourself and for your father, see him as a human being—like you are. Do you know that you did not deserve any shaming criticism you experienced as a boy? You didn't deserve it, in case you don't know the answer. No one deserves to be shamed, and that includes your father. That doesn't mean that people don't deserve to be confronted, questioned, or challenged, or that you don't owe it to yourself to confront, question, or challenge your father. There is a difference between these and shaming or attacking, however. The attitude, the method, and the desired outcome are different. Ask yourself, am I doing what I am doing with this person because I think it will make things better, deeper, more beautiful, or do I want them to hurt, be in pain, suffer—is my goal to see his blood spill? Is that the final outcome I want?

Shaming and revenge—these are the tools of the impotent, the weak, and the stupid. They have no place in the acts of the masculine. They can be recognized as natural impulses, whose purpose is to awaken our inner being and reveal our intensity of feelings. This energy can be expressed—through unsent letters, artwork, fantasy, dreams, and then transformed in the relationship as a motivating energy source, part of the depth of our archetypal desire for a connection between son and father.

These suggestions hold true, by the way, for all relationships, not only that between son and father. It is more useful to approach someone with a respectful and compassionate attitude. In the case of the son's compassion for the father, it has to do with the very good possibility that his father simply didn't know how to be a father to him. He didn't learn how from his own father—no one taught him. Let us hope that we, as fathers to our own sons, can reintroduce the attention to the father–son relationship as a primary foundation of a connection to each other, to other people, and to the natural world.

The most useful attitude, then, is one of exploration, one of contacting your own pain and your own grief, and attempting a reconciliation that has the possibility of adding creatively to your life, rather than piling on new hurts, and new destructions. All the more reason why we originally suggested that you do preliminary or preparatory work. It will allow for the release of a lot of intense emotions, which include anger, blaming, and resentment. By releasing the rage or intensity earlier, the son can approach his father without blowing up like a loose cannon.

A metaphor I often use is the image of two baskets. In one basket is all of the old material, the resentments and leftover pain in relationships with family, friends, and others. These are things that need attention, they are still gnawing at and affecting relationships, thinking, and behavior. These things need attending to over time, perhaps years and years, and even a whole lifetime. In another basket there exists the desire to have a good current relationship with family and friends. The basket holds a sincere longing for and a very necessary sense of connection—even though many of those you wish to connect with may have been or are hurtful with you. This second basket, filled with desires for a family connection, may need to be ignored for a while if the family is, or could be, abusive or hurtful today. To reconcile old hurts and new, deeper, more intimate relationships, you need first to discriminate between the two baskets. You can be working on old resentments and old hurts over in one basket, while maintaining a relationship with others, with family in particular, though this principle applies as well to old friendships.

One good example is holiday get-togethers. This is *never* a good time to get out the contents of the first basket, the basket of old resentments and old pains. This is a time to work on the maintenance of the ongoing, current relationship with the family. It is much more effective to arrange other, nonholiday times for getting together with family members, individually or as a group, to work through old pain. The right time for you as an individual to initiate this process is when you have a clear understanding of your own feelings and thoughts, and of whatever your own contribution to any problems in the past might have been. Work on yourself first, then initiate with others. Your own clarity will help you stay out of old muddles. You will not be so reactive as you might have once been, since you can identify what is happening with you and with your family better. One suggestion is to work through this book, do the exercises, try some of the resources listed in the back, and then initiate the resolution of old issues with your family.

Both of these baskets, both of these areas of your life, require attention. Neither one is more primary; each requires the other. Everyone needs to work either simultaneously or in sequence on these two baskets, in order to develop, to have intimacy, and to solve problems in life. If the focus gets too heavily weighted on the basket of old resentments, you forget to work on your relationships today. If you work entirely on the basket of current relationships, and forget to take care of the archaic aspects of your life, those resentments will inevitably creep in to harm you in your current relationships.

In terms of working on reconciliation with your father, it's important to remember that old resentments, old pains, and old grief need attention and work. Your current relationship also needs attention and work. What this means is that you may be able to do certain kinds of activities, have certain kinds of involvements with your father before everything old or archaic is worked out and understood. As your father is getting older, so are you. How much longer will he be alive? You have an opportunity to get to know each other now—maybe you haven't known each other all these forty or fifty years. Why not start now? This way you won't lose the opportunity to know your father as he is now—as we mentioned, he may be quite different from when you were growing up. Nor will you lose the opportunity to contact and make meaning and importance of your own personal history.

The bottom line: reconciliation is not a one-shot event. It is not girding yourself to confront another person; there are aspects of confrontation involved, but reconciliation is mostly alternate and intermittent dipping into one basket or the other. On some occasions, one basket is more appropriate than the other. Reconciliation is a long-term proposition that occurs over time. It occurs in the context of multiple relationships. It occurs against the backdrop of dealing with what was and integrating that with what is now.

Construction of a Family Map

Unless someone in your family has gone to a lot of trouble to write a family history and draw a family tree, or has been conscientious about making sure you know your relatives and their personal stories, you probably don't have a very good "picture" of all the relationships in the last couple of generations of your family. Most American families have lost a sense of contact and continuity with their family history. If you have the information readily available, and have a good sense of it, you are in a good position to know more about some of your own patterns of thinking, feeling, and acting. This claim is made on the basis of extensive current theory which demonstrates that families create patterns or ways of coping with stress, closeness, and distance; success or failure in education, finances and work; and intensity and frequency of illness, among other things. These patterns are developed over many, many generations, and influence each new member of a family in profound ways, many of which are not consciously recognized.

A "family map" can demonstrate a wide-ranging family perspective; like any map, this design can give you immediate and graphic information about who is connected to whom, what these connections suggest, and what events are likely to take place at certain crucial ages in the lives of family members—like death, illness, marriage, failure at a business—unless there is major intervention or change.

The theory behind the family map suggests that when someone dies, marries, divorces, has a child, enters the hospital, or has other important life events, all members of the family in the current generation are affected in one way or another, and members of consecutive generations are subtly or not so subtly influenced by these events as well. The family map, which links one generation to the next, can help you understand how indicators in relationships, such as closeness or distance between family members, can be indicators of problems that may influence your life now, but be the fruit of foundations laid many generations ago. What follows is the map for a three-generation family, the Sheldons. We will show you this one, and then ask you to make one of your own family.

The Sheldons are a middle-class family living in a suburb of a large metropolitan area. The parents, Jeff and Molly, are both employed with good jobs. Jeff's history of employment has been erratic, with many job changes, but he has stayed in his current position for three years. Molly, on the other hand, has a solid job history, rising through the ranks in a national department store chain. Part of the ongoing marital conflict between them has focused upon Jeff's losing or changing jobs. The children, Julie and Mike, are both teenagers. Julie is a very responsible, model child, a good student involved in many school activities. Mike, however, has had a long history of low school performance, requiring tutors and additional in-school support. His learning difficulties have caused a certain amount of worry and anxiety for both parents, with Jeff feeling perturbed and frustrated with Mike for what he sees as the boy's lack of proper motivation in school.

As you can see, this family has had some difficulties but has remained together and achieved a certain level of stability. The parents, Jeff and Molly, remain in contact with their own families of origin. Each has developed a career. Though success with Mike has not resulted from their attention to his problems yet, the parents remain hopeful and confident that a solution will be reached. Even with these positive signs, the Sheldons are a family affected by problems with functioning in their own lives and similar problems from their extended families of origin. The context of relationship patterns has been operating for several generations.

The figure on the next page shows you the Sheldon family map, which you can use as a model for diagramming

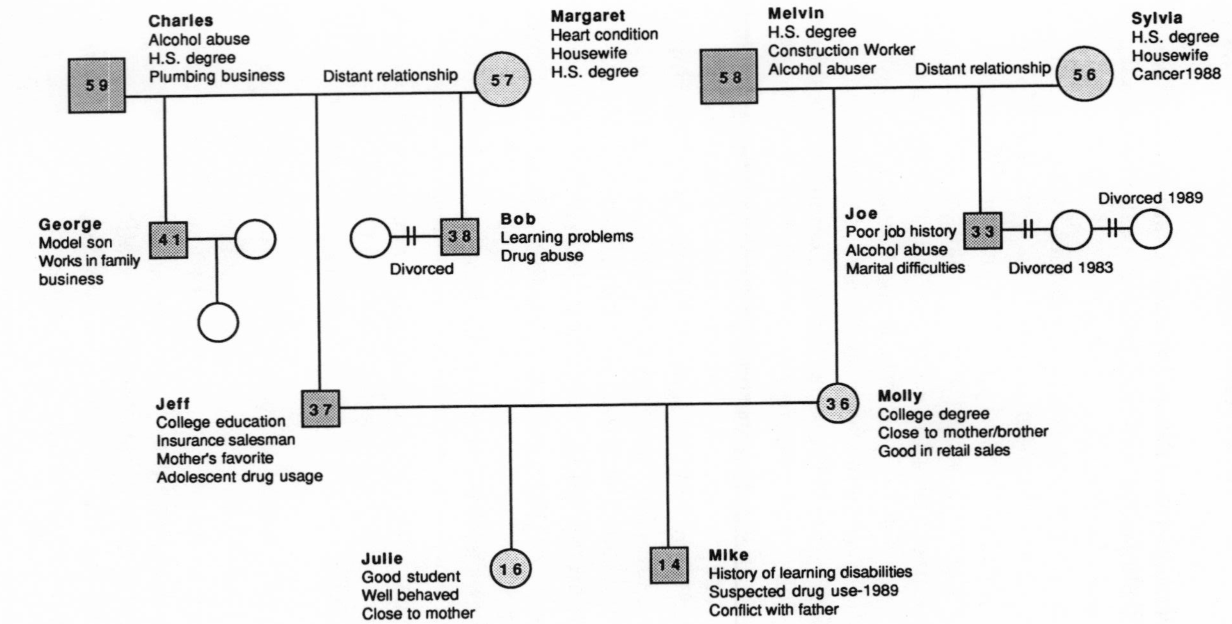

Sheldon family map. The map reads from top (oldest generation) to bottom (youngest). A box indicates a male, a circle a female. Lines between the two indicate marriages, and then below the marriage, children, who are listed from left to right in order of their birth sequence.

your own. The Sheldon's map allows us to discuss how patterns of functioning in this family influence their lives. You will be able to view your own family through the model offered by this multigenerational map, and identify both the positive and unhealthy patterns in your family that are portrayed.

The Sheldon's map contains the following information about where problems might arise in this family:

1. History of alcohol and drug abuse on both sides of family.
2. Oldest child being responsible and goal directed.
3. Second-born male using drugs and having learning problems.
4. Adolescence appears to be a high-risk time for this family, when school and drug problems emerge.
5. Youngest men appear to be either someone's favorite (coddled and protected by mother or sister) or someone's disappointment (fighting with father).
6. Marriage partnerships on both sides of family marked by distance and lack of closeness; divorce in the next generation.
7. Substance abuse and marital difficulties linked together with sons taking the brunt of family problems.
8. Fathers and sons distant and in conflict with each other, with sons overinvolved with their mothers and ultimately less intimate with their wives.

Get a good-sized piece of paper. Poster size is best, so you can write as much information as possible. Using the Sheldon family map as a model, begin drawing your own diagram, using the following symbols:

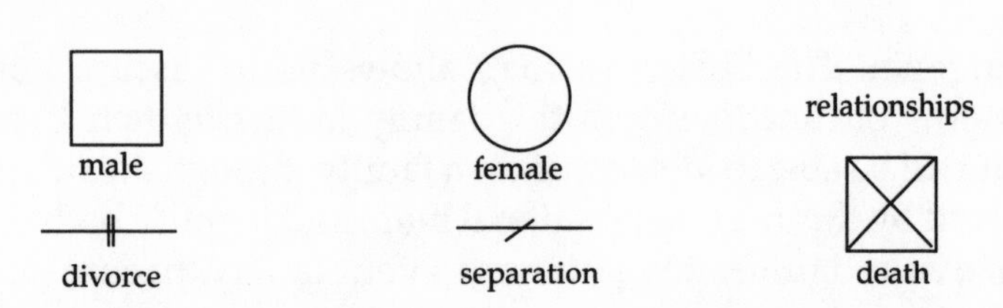

Start with your current family and work backwards, several generations if possible. Work and school history, educational attainment, and health information should be noted. If possible, list the dates of any important occurrences (births, deaths, divorces, major achievements of any kind), since the timing of events often triggers an increase in family anxiety, or signals a significant change in the family.

Once you have finished drawing your map, stand back and look at it. What do you see as you look at it? Notice any feelings, thoughts, memories, and body sensations that occur to you.

Here are some additional questions for you to consider:

- How would you characterize your current family relationships? Who is close or distant with whom? Does anybody get a "favorite" position with anybody else?
- What kinds of achievements have been made by members of the family, educationally, in work, sports, creative endeavors, or in other areas?
- Do any members of the family abuse substances such as alcohol or drugs, or have other patterns of addiction?
- What similarities or differences do you see in any of the above ways between your immediate family and the generation before you, that is, your grandparents and your aunts and uncles?
- In your extended family as a whole, how do people

relate to one another? Are there family reunions or other get-togethers? Are there family grudges or deep resentments that are unresolved? What are the people involved doing about this problem?

- When problems emerge in your family at large, do people tend to "pull together" or "go it alone?" Do people lean on others too much, refuse to ask for help, or seem to have a balanced and reasonable attitude in asking for help from each other?
- Do you and your children (if you have any) relate to both sides of the family, yours and your partners? Is there contact with grandparents, aunts, uncles, cousins? What benefit have you seen from this contact?
- Look carefully at the men in your extended family. What patterns do you see in education, in work, in addictions, in health, and in relationships with one another?

In practical terms, we can mention that for men—at least at this moment in our cultural and psychological evolution—what bears meaning is not words and not emotions, but actions. Whether that is right or wrong, we don't really know. But it is true. For men, friendships and relationships with other men and women are based on the virtue of action—the quality of action and the judgment of that action. Does he or she deliver, or not?

Men value an activity done together more than any exchange of words. That is perhaps even truer of men in their sixties, seventies, and eighties. What this means for adult sons is that initiating a relationship with your father means more than working through some things. It means starting up some kind of activity, even a nonessential one, you can do together. There are many men who will not work on the basket of old relationships; it is too threatening, they just won't do it. For them the basket of today is all that is going to get their attention. These men, as well as the others who are looking at both baskets, can engage their fathers in similar ways. Try to find activities that both of you enjoy. Though you both might not find the activity equal in innate pleasure, each of you will find out more about why the other one likes it and why it is important to him. Should you both have common interests, so much the better.

We are encouraging families of men, especially if there are several generations of men within the family, to begin to look at ways they can connect on a basis meaningful for all of them. If you have a number of male siblings, are there ways that you and your brothers can spend time doing something together? Perhaps you will include your dad sometimes, and sometimes not. If your father has died, you can still "include" him in a way by referring to him and to your relationship with him whenever you get together with your brothers or uncles or other family members. His influence is still alive with all of you.

A three-generational get-together of men is a powerhouse of energy! An unbelievable amount of psychic, emotional, and physical power accumulates when several generations of men gather together. Families of men getting together can be valuable and exciting. Grandfather, father, and son engaged in an intergenerational activity is a moment of history.

When my brothers, father, and I get together and do something, this sets up not only something in our own family for the moment in which it happens, but an event which can affect generations of boys to come, and—perhaps on a limited but meaningful basis—even give a nudge to the culture and development of men throughout the culture. We can get back something lost, which existed in other cultures. When you get together, do it in a way that begins to establish or reestablish a kind of ceremony, a meaningful activity, a ritual of connection among men. This will lead to a greater cohesiveness as well as an appreciation for the company of men.

The reconciliation of fathers and sons is not only a reconciliation in the nuclear family, but a rejoining and linking of the generations of fathers and sons, a building of community among men. This is also a beginning of reconciliation not only with our emotional natures, but with our connection to other people, to the places where we live, to nature, and to the planet we live on. When we respect and find within our family and friends a model for understanding and compassion, this begins to lead to a model of compassion not only for other people but for the natural world as well.

Earlier we mentioned that the adult son who is considering his connection with his father has the responsibility to begin to initiate a reconciliation with him. The same process is applicable to the older father who now is looking at his relationship with his adult son and is realizing that it has been, and is currently, a relationship he hasn't thought much about or given much of himself to. The father's initiation of reconciliation can certainly take many of the same forms that we explored with the adult son. Again, preliminary and preparatory work, hard inner work, needs to be done. But in being a father, it will take a slightly different form. You can make a special call just to him. You can be responsible for obtaining time with him alone. When birthday cards, holiday greetings, or the like are sent, often it is the mother who sends them; go ahead and send one on your own! It seems like a simple thing, but be aware of your response as you consider it. Do you reject it right away, or perhaps say, of course, I'll do that, I just didn't think of it before?

Now as a father, you may have some of the same "first-basket" resentments or angers or frustrations with your son leftover from the days when he was younger. Maybe he rejected you and didn't allow you to have the kind of relationship you really wanted to have. When you did make time for him, did he want nothing to do with you? Did he speak ill of you, calling you and your work stupid or crass or evil? You naturally had a reaction to that. You might ask, what right does he have to get your attention now after that kind of behavior? Well, do you or don't you want to know your son before you die? Now consider: what kind of relationship did you have with your own father? Aren't there some similarities? Can you remember what you longed for from him? That is, likely, what your own son feels as a longing from you as well.

Then there are grandfathers. The grandfather is one of the most underrated and underused resources going. Here is a guy who has been around the block for a number of years, has the family blood and history flowing in his veins. His rich complexity of years of experience, conflicts, thoughts, fantasies, and emotions cannot be duplicated. And grandfathers can have the most wonderful relationships with their grandsons. They have far fewer encumbrances, like jobs, eating up their time. If the father has any sense, he should encourage the grandfather to have a good, enjoyable relationship with his grandson. The boy can learn about old age, about experience (grandpa, remember not to preach!), about history, about the family, about his own body's future; the grandfather can relive and bring up his own latent boyhood (he's freer now, one hopes, to be more childlike than in his most fervent career years) and revivify some of the excitement, joys, griefs, pains, hopes, and dreams of young boys.

A connection between the grandfather and grandson also opens the door for the father to talk with his son—and with his own father—about their relationships, about dilemmas that arise from being a parent. Grandfathers can cite a time when the father was behaving just like the grandson and how the grandfather dealt with it then. This is a good entree for excavating parts of the relationship, both positive and negative and to learn from the past for the future.

Just as there had been a cultural image established of the older father as untrustworthy, what can begin to grow now is the cultural importance of the father as an active family member. There is now a generation of men who have been raised with the expectation of greater involvement by the father. Fatherhood and father–son relationships have taken on sweeping importance in men's lives today. This enables the grandfather to initiate with his grandson a connection with the freedom and enjoyment the adult son and his father may never have realized. This can open up a new set of possibilities of the adult son and father learning to know each other as well. Moreover, the adult son—now a father—has the opportunity to practice and show his son, and his own father, through his actions, what he believes to be important.

We mentioned that adult sons need to realize that their fathers might have difficulty understanding the son's interest in this new movement toward reconciliation. By the same token, what the older father needs to realize about his middle-aged son is that his son grew up at a time when he was instructed continuously and had good reason to mistrust older men. Men now thirty-five to fifty years old were alive during the Vietnam era, as teens or older. One of the things they discovered again and again was that the older men lied to them a great deal. Our involvement in Vietnam was distorted through the reportage we were allowed to know: the number of young men who were dying—men their own age—was deliberately downplayed; the information about the reasons for our involvement was calculated more for elusive business ends than for the sake of a deep commitment to our values. The philosophy for the young men (and women) of the era was summed up in the motto—remember this?—"Don't trust anyone over thirty."

Also, most fathers of that generation were simply not available to their sons. The sons had little access to their fathers, and were instructed to have little to do with them. Fathers were expected to work hard and be left alone to read the newspaper when they came home.

Because of the political atmosphere at that time, as well as the traditional domestic conventions expected of mom and dad, there was a sanctioned mistrust and hatred toward older men. Although this may have been submerged as the younger men grew older themselves, there always remains a residue of experience, emotion, and memory. One result is that the adult sons—now over thirty themselves—don't trust their fathers, and they don't trust themselves, either. Many of the Vietnam radicals have turned "right wing," in fact, and are some of the more distinctly conservative citizens. This might lead to a "double" or "triple mistrust" by middle-aged men: a mistrust of father, of self, and of the young sons. So there is a lot to work on.

The older father who is hoping to initiate a reconciliation should likely expect mistrust and suspicion from his son. In the same way we cautioned adult sons to be respectful of their older fathers slowly making themselves emotionally available, we also caution older fathers against expecting to be immediately embraced, accepted, and forgiven by your adult son.

Again we reiterate our encouragement and hope that in any reconciliation between fathers and sons, the primary method employed is an attitude of respectfulness and understanding about the messages of manhood, power, and competency that were current at the time that each of us came into manhood.

A respectful approach means attempting to understand the world through the eyes of another. For adult sons, this means an attempt to understand the way the father views manhood. For the older father it means an attempt to understand the way the adult son perceives, knows, and frames his world in terms of being a man. Adopting this kind of open-minded attitude is a good start.

Chapter 13

Father's Blessing

The protagonist of the movie *Field of Dreams* plows up a burgeoning corn crop on his financially beseiged farm in Iowa and builds a major league style baseball diamond, all on the inspiration of a voice he hears in the field that says to him, "If you build it, he will come." He is challenged to pursue an elusive (some would call it "insane") dream on the strength of deeply felt intuition and hope for fulfillment and satisfaction. Through his crusade to construct the ball field, he rediscovers fortitude, courage, and perseverance. These were attributes which he was in danger of losing; he was at the point of giving up hope that he would ever feel these things again in his life. He also resolves his long-standing estrangement with his dead father, a baseball player, who reappears to him with other famous ball players, in the field the protagonist builds. The movie ends with the fulfillment of his longing to meet his father again and feel his father's pride in him, and to receive his father's blessing.

We opened this book by challenging men to begin a search for understanding of themselves and other men. We offered a similarly elusive promise to the challenge offered in the movie, "If you build it he will come." Our promise is that if you rebuild your relationship with your father—and with other men, women, and with your own inner self—you will find a deep satisfaction you may not have known before.

We stated in the beginning and throughout the book that the process of building long-lasting and intimate relationships can be arduous, and requires sacrifice of time, effort, and possibly money to achieve. Rewards will come to those men willing to reflect on their lives, seek help from others, and make the behavioral changes necessary to alter a lifetime of habits. Many men experience discontent, isolation, and confusion in the areas of their lives we describe in this book. They often work and play without pleasure or joy; their achievements are finally unsatisfying; they use addictions of many kinds to attempt some masking of emotional pain, but that results in its opposite—more suffering; they lack intimate connections with other people with whom they can participate deeply in the pleasures and sufferings of life; they die lonely, afraid, and empty.

A key to their despair is the missing crucial connection in their lives: a solid father–son relationship. A meaningful connection between the generations of men is built on a lifetime of contact, sustained interest, and attention to each person's contribution to the relationship. The contribution of such things as money, good schools, occasional support for sports or good grades will not in themselves result in the kind of intimacy that is possible between parents and children. A father must give of himself—his time, attention, loyalty, physical presence, and commitment to be present in his son's life. The son, in turn, must be ready to take from his father, to receive what he has to offer, to challenge or accuse him of wrongdoings he sees; and then as an adult, to initiate time with his father, to attend to the relationship between the two, and to seek resolution of whatever pain or grief may be left over from his childhood. Each must do his part to make this relationship alive, changing, and deepening.

The father is like a diving board to his young son. His son uses his force to spring out into the world. The son keeps coming back again and again, climbing up and jumping again. The role of the father is to support his son and give him a push into the world, and to let the son make the right moves for himself, that is, what moves he chooses to make and what achievements he chooses to undertake in life. Sometimes the son will bellyflop, and other times, he will gracefully turn over, around, and down, and enter the water gracefully.

With a deep relationship with his father as a base and springboard, the son is ready to meet the complexities he encounters outside the family. He can choose a profession that fulfills and brings pleasure. He can choose close friends at work and in other activities, and have a sense of what it takes to be a good friend with other men. A son who carries a model of a loving, healthy relationship between his father and mother inside himself can choose a partner to love and spend time with in mutual development of a life together. He will have a strong advantage in the challenging process of raising children. A son raised by a father who honestly and forthrightly confronts and assesses his own values and morals and those of others can confidently take on the task of his own commitments in life.

We close this book with a strong sense of hope for men in their relationships with others. This hope is borne out for us daily in our clinical practice, in our talks with men around the nation, and in our own lives. A powerful change in our definitions and experience of maleness is happening, and increasing numbers of men are wanting to be a part of this change.

It was almost unthinkable for men two generations ago to sit together in a room and express their longing for their fathers, for deep friendships, for greater intimacy with their wives, or for joy and excitement at work. Yet today, this is happening all across the nation, and in various parts of the world, in men's groups.

There have always been men who risked intimacy, directness, and joyfulness in their lives. For them, this "men's movement" is nothing new, but what they have practiced already. However, such men have been in a minority and continuously bucking the "standard definition" of manhood. These men are alive in our culture and we should assiduously seek them out.

For many men, however, there is a sense of adventure in discovering and exploring their lives as men and as emotional beings. This is a new possibility, an opportunity to find self and community, to break the barriers of isolation and loneliness. Some science fiction writers have described the fantasy of another world overlayed on our world which by clever technological tricks we might discover. Reality is even more fantastic. All we have to do is pay attention to ourselves, to our relationships, and to our own family patterns and we can discover a new world that really does exist and is available to us.

Some men we talk with have been discouraged by this talk of change. The feel they have done something irreparably wrong in the way they have lived their lives before. Some fathers think that their parenting has permanently crippled their sons. Some sons think that since they didn't have the father they needed, there is little hope for them to "be whole." Others feel that a life-long pattern of isolation now "curses" them to remain cut off since they don't know another way.

If you are among these discouraged ones, or feel discouraged in these ways at times, take heart. First of all, you do have the tools you need to break out of your isolation or loneliness or addictions. You just need to learn how to use them. That is what this book is all about, discovering how to use the tools you already have. These tools are thinking, feeling, and awareness of your body. Some of them are rusty or have been used little, but you do have them and can use them with practice.

Second, you are not alone and you don't have to be alone in your work on yourself. This statement is increasingly valid. Everywhere we look, men's groups are springing up, at churches, at universities, in community centers. If there is not one in your area, get a few guys together, give them copies of this book or others, and start a group of your own.

Third, many of the things you already do and have already done are *just fine.* Throughout the book, we have focused many of our exercises on recapturing and bringing to awareness your own personal history, your already existing connections with your family and friends. We have focused on taking what you already have and appreciating its value, on using your currently existing resources. Our message is: deepen and enrich what is there before you at this moment. Know your family history. Know your history with friends. Recognize addictive behavior. Seek joy and meaning in what is present to you each day.

The Blessing

Freeman stood on the front porch, looking out at the pickup loaded with boxes, a bicycle, and a few sticks of furniture. He had landed what he called "a great job" with Bright Rivers Company, which specialized in Environmental Reclamation. He was going to work specifically in stream rebuilding and reclaiming. He had always loved the outdoors, and during his college summers had worked for the conservation department of each of four states. But Freeman was full of anger at this moment. He and his parents had been arguing for months, through the spring semester of his senior year, about his job choice.

His parents did little to hide their disappointment in Freeman. His father, Roger, was senior partner in one of the best law firms in the city. He had hoped since Freeman's birth that one day they would practice law together. Now he was going off to what seemed like a "glorified summer job." Freeman's mother, Elizabeth, was a marketing director for a national TV network. She also had hoped that Freeman would become an attorney, and eventually go into politics to effect change in environmental policy, and use television in a meaningful way.

At this moment, on the porch, ready to leave, what Freeman hoped for more than anything was that his parents—particularly his father—would understand his decision, be proud of him for doing what he felt was right, and give him their blessing. He was certain it would not happen like he hoped it would. He knew his parents were disappointed. He knew just as well that he was making the right decision for himself. Even though inside him there was a deep sadness about leaving his parents with this rift between them, he was mostly aware of anger. He was enraged and righteous about his decision. Even if both of his parents had come out right at that moment and told him from the bottom of their hearts that they supported his decision, he was not about to accept a thing from them!

How hard it is to give a blessing, and how hard to receive one. We see in this vignette a moment in the life of a young man and his parents when things are ripe for a celebration of accomplishment and a send-off for Freeman into a life of his own. Why is it so difficult to simply give a blessing to another person? Why is it so painful to give to our own flesh and blood the blessing we know they need? Why is it so painful to receive such a blessing?

Perhaps the reason is that blessing another person or being blessed means a deep, unconditional acceptance of a human being's inherent value, regardless of their actions, behavior, or attitude. In fact, when we look at the original meaning of the word *blessing,* we find that it means "sacrificing," sacrificing our will and egotism to something deeper and greater than ourselves. The word *bless* comes from the Old English word which means "blood." To bless meant to consecrate, to recognize as holy. The mark of blessing was blood, the very seat and sign of life. We can see from this that to bless or be blessed means something which goes to the very core of our being.

If you give your blessing to another man, you are saying that you accept his inherent value. This is not something done lightly, but if it were to be done even on a small scale, the effects would be profound. When a father blesses a son with a deep acceptance, that blessing goes in on the level of the blood. Few other things are as powerful for a man in his own life, or as deeply desired and needed by him. The level of true confidence (not cockiness) that is shown by a man blessed by his father is something that shines through in all of his acts, thoughts, and feelings. We have a rich masculine heritage to learn from, and at the same time, many things we wish to change. Our heritage is a blessing.

To bless another person or to be blessed is not something acquired easily or lightly. It cannot be really achieved in a weekend workshop, although one can get a glimmer of what it might be like. It is a bloody, messy matter, accomplished through daily attention to your relationships with others and with yourself. The sense of being blessed is accomplished in small ways over time. It is accomplished by attention to equality in your relationships with other men, women, and children. It is accomplished by establishing a strong understanding and emotional tie to your family history, by reconciliation with your father. It is accomplished by attention to the values you demonstrate with others in your job and by attention to political and social issues. Blessing is accomplished by deepening your own inner life and by attention to spiritual development. This is the message and hope of our book.

May we bless one another.

Chapter 14

More Resources for Men

Therapy

What is therapy? Do I need it? What can I get out of it?

From the birth of modern psychotherapy with the work of psychiatrists Joseph Breuer and Sigmund Freud 100 years ago, the great majority of people who have sought therapy have been women. Recently, however, ever-increasing numbers of men have been getting therapy of their own. They have gone to therapy perhaps begrudingly in many cases, under the duress of wives, friends, or court mandates, but they have nonetheless started turning up in mental health workers' offices. And an increasing number are going because they *want to and choose to do so.*

Why do they go? Why and when would someone choose to enter therapy? We suspect that many men don't go to therapy because the situation looks too daunting and unfamiliar. It is our hope to somewhat demystify the process in order to make it more understandable for men who might consider it.

There has been greater permission in recent American culture for women to talk about personal things with other people. But many men can hardly imagine it. How many models have we had of grown men sitting down with one another and talking about personal issues? How many of you remember your father talking for an hour (or five minutes, even) about something deeply personal—his fears, his sadness, or his private religious experience? Very few, we venture to guess. Nonetheless, some things have changed. More men feel comfortable about seeking therapy than in the past. Many men are deciding to take risks with each other to talk personally and frankly. Many fathers now are working hard to change old patterns of distance and detachment.

So let's assume that you have identified some issues you think you might wish to work on in therapy, if you were to go. You believe you *might* get something out of it, though you are not sure what. Perhaps someone you know claims he was helped, which encourages you. But you are not sure what you can expect to happen in a therapy session or what you might hope for.

Let's discuss how to choose a therapist, when to seek therapy, and what results you might reasonably expect. Those of you who have been in therapy (or therapists) could skip this section, since it will likely be rudimentary to you, or you could read it to see if you agree or disagree with our view of therapy and therapists. Your experience might be similar or very different from our description.

One good way to choose a therapist is to get a referral from an acquaintance who has had a good experience in therapy. Beyond that, you might consider a referral from your family physician, although frankly, some physicians are not very well informed about therapy. Another good way to "get a look" at therapists is to sign up for workshops or seminars offered by them. Many therapists offer such events both as an opportunity for teaching and as advertisement. You can go to one of these events and get a "feel" of the therapist without having to take the step of sitting down one-on-one with him.

In any case, if you do call a therapist, make it clear that you are "interviewing" him to see if you want to work with him. Ask lots of questions, anything that occurs to you. If you have a positive experience talking to him on the phone, ask for an initial interview in person. It is much better to meet in person, to find out if you like being in his presence, if you believe you can trust him, and if things feel "right" about his approach with you.

You will have to decide whether to work with a male or female therapist. Many men feel more comfortable talking with women about their personal lives. This can be a good reason for choosing a woman, because a trusting, positive, working relationship contributes a good deal to the therapy process. Some men have had trouble trusting women, and the experience of working with a woman can be very useful in working with your sense of trust. One thought on this subject is to work for a period of time with a female therapist and then with a male therapist and find out for yourself which you prefer. Ideally you could work with either a male or female and work on resolving any issue. In practice, it usually turns out that we have different reactions to men than we do to women. Being aware of and talking about these differences can be very helpful in your discovery of your assumptions, thoughts, and feelings toward men and toward women.

Before you meet with any therapist, do some homework. Think about what it is you would like to get out of therapy. Try to be as specific as you can. "I would like to feel less anxious when I speak in public" is better than "I'd like to be more comfortable." It is a very good idea to write down what you think your issues or problems are and what you would like to get out of therapy. This step can help you and your therapist greatly and very possibly save time and money.

As therapists, we have found that many men come to discuss a number of the issues listed below. Perhaps some of these apply to you:

- Dissatisfaction with friendships with other men, or failure to make other than casual acquaintances.
- Dissatisfaction with marriage or family life.
- "Bottled up" rage that you don't know what to do with or are expressing inappropriately through hostility or violence.
- Lack of confidence in your job; poor work performance or dissatisfaction with your work.
- Desire to change careers, and needing help in how to do so.
- Problems with a child's behavior at home, in school, or with peer relationships.
- Problems with drugs or alcohol.
- Fatigue not due to a medical reason.
- Stress-related illnesses.
- Difficulty talking with family members, friends, coworkers.
- Lack of enjoyment in life.

The discussions in therapy mainly focus on three basic categories of problems: (1) the particular problems, as the ones above, that you wish to work on; (2) your inability thus far to solve the problem through various approaches; (3) how having this problem makes you feel or think about yourself. Your therapist will most probably work with you on each of these categories. In some ways, number 3 is the cornerstone for many men, since their self-image may suffer if they need to ask another person to help. Interestingly, this is the very block which hampers their development the most. If you have permission to be human—that is, to have problems from time to time—it is much easier to take charge of yourself and be effective in changing.

Again, if you go to a therapist for any one of these or other reasons, be sure to be specific with him about what you have noticed about yourself. Try to define the problems as carefully as you can. If you are experiencing "lack of enjoyment in life," for example, ask yourself: In what areas of my life do I lack enjoyment—work, family life, friendships? How would I like things to be for me?

Don't be surprised if you find yourself in therapy working on a problem that is not the one you came in for, however. Many times what we are conscious of, for example, anger at a spouse, is a symptom and simply the most obvious manifestation of a more basic underlying problem. In this example, it could be anger at women due to a series of bad experiences in relationships, or it could be the result of many other experiences in life.

One initial assignment we often use in therapy is to ask people to write a short autobiography (three to five pages), highlighting important points in their lives, people who have influenced them, accomplishments and decisions they have made. A similar assignment is a "time line," going from the day of birth to the present moment, with important events marked on the time line, and a vertical graph for marking whether each event was experienced as very "positive" or "negative."

In the first session, continue asking questions of the therapist. Ask him about his approach to therapy, how he works, how he conducts sessions. Ask him if he has had experience working with men (many have not had much), and if he has worked with the particular problems you are bringing to him. How long has he been practicing? Also, it is all right to ask him if he has any *personal* experience with the problems you are working on. While some therapists will answer that question, others will not. Some think it makes a difference and others do not. Our opinion is that it is not *necessary* for the therapist to have had similar experiences to be able to help you, but it can add a dimension of depth and understanding if he has had similar experiences. Nonetheless, it also sometimes results in less objectivity by the therapist about your problems. A good therapist will be aware of his own issues and/or biases, and will have worked on them to have achieved some personal resolution.

Ask about his credentials. There are all kinds of credentials and all kinds of backgrounds that therapists have. Ask him to explain to you what his credentials mean in relation to his approach to working with people in therapy. Some therapists are more oriented to a "medical model" and put emphasis on psychiatric diagnosis and drugs. Some rely on testing and behavioral change. Others are more strongly oriented to family systems and their influence on us, or to addiction treatment, insight and personal growth, or spiritual development. Some put more emphasis on individual treatment and some are adamant about groups. Each of these, and many other, approaches have contributed to the field of psychotherapy, and a good therapist from most of these orientations can help you in his own way of doing therapy. Find out what your therapist's approach is.

Credentials in themselves do not guarantee competence, and certainly do not promise that a therapist will be right for you. The vast majority of what goes into making a good therapist is learned long after graduate school, in postgraduate training and in experience working with people, as well as in personal maturation. It is believed by many theoreticians and practitioners that a therapist cannot take a client beyond where he himself has developed, and there is some truth in that.

Ask about the therapist's fee, the frequency of appointments, and any other business matters (such as insurance) as soon as possible in the first session. Don't be afraid to negotiate on the fee. A fee can be negotiated in various ways: some (not all) therapists have sliding scales according to income; you might negotiate the frequency of visits to a number which meets your household budget. Some insurance companies will co-pay for visits to therapists, depending on many factors. You can consult your company about this. But you should know that using insurance for therapy might possibly have an effect on your future insurability, and that for insurance companies to pay, they require a psychiatric diagnosis. You may want to consider whether you would want that information available—and such information is increasingly available to many parties. Talk over the effect that making insurance claims may have on you and on the therapy with your therapist, and make sure you understand what the implications are before you make the decision whether to use insurance.

Then ask the therapist what you might reasonably expect to get from therapy with him, given the problems you are bringing and the approach he has. Some therapists focus on defining precise behavioral problems and contracting for change in those areas. Others are more oriented to a general, deep change in life patterns, or even to self-understanding and consciousness, regardless of whether immediate change takes place. What is it you want? It might be obvious to you that therapy oriented to general, deep change in long-standing life patterns will probably take longer and be more of a commitment on your part than changing one or two behaviors. However, not everyone is in need of such sweeping changes.

The rate of change you experience during therapy will be influenced strongly by numerous things in addition to the competence of your therapist. Among them may be such things as:

- How long you have had the problem(s).
- If you are in a supportive environment (family, friends, work).
- How high your motivation for change is.
- Your dedication to participate actively in the therapy.
- How good your working relationship with your therapist is.
- Your physical health.

Many people describe feeling a little better even after their first therapy session. This in, in part, because they have decided to do something about a problem that may have been bothering them for a long time, sometimes even ten or twenty years or more. Just that act of recognizing that there is a problem to be worked on, and your doing something constructive about it, can send the strong message to yourself that you believe things can be better for you.

Men in particular are notoriously bad about asking for help, though they get solid competition in this area from some women, who are similarly hesitant to ask for help. If you are reluctant to ask for help, we don't blame you. We appreciate any skepticism you might have. In fact, we encourage you to experience your doubts about the therapy process and put your therapist to the test by asking all the questions you might have. From the first session onward, you should be putting your doubts and misgivings right on the table. When you express these doubts honestly, you give yourself and your therapist an opportunity to work things through. If you hide your thoughts and feelings, you won't get the help you came for.

Many of the exercises we suggest throughout the book can help you get in touch with your thoughts and feelings as well as awareness of your body. One of the things you can do in therapy is to learn to use this information coming from yourself to help you find and maintain better relationships with other people. For example, if you feel strong anger or even rage when you practice an exercise in describing how you felt with your father, you can find out in therapy how to express this anger in safe and constructive ways. If you did the exercises in the book and registered no feelings, that too is something to work on with your therapist.

Everyone has the capability to be more intimate and more satisfied in his relationships than he is at the present moment. Everyone has the capacity to be less anxious and more confident, creative, self-aware, self-revealing, and intimate with other people. The tools are available in each person. These skills can be learned and practiced. Therapy is one place to work on developing yourself in these ways.

It can be frightening as well as exciting to learn more about yourself as well as to change. You may experience conflicting feelings. On one hand, you may feel some darkness and terror inside you; on the other hand, you might also feel exuberance and joy. Therapy can be very hard work, but it can also be a fascinating and regenerating experience. We believe that the vast majority of men and women could benefit from some therapy during their lives, and would like to see it available to many more people than currently have access to a therapist.

We hope that this brief discussion has helped make the experience of therapy seem less formidable and more useful to those of you who have considered getting some professional help for yourselves.

Chapter 15

More Resources for Men

Groups and Group Exercises

Groups

Involvement in a group provides the opportunity to work on many of the issues we have addressed in this book. The group experience can offer a sense of belonging, of loyalty, of commitment to a common purpose. Groups offer the chance to laugh, play, cry, heal emotional wounds, joke, tell stories from your life, get support, pull together with others toward a goal, and confront others or be confronted by others on self-destructive behaviors. They can offer an antidote to the loneliness and isolation many men report.

But what kind of group would be of interest to you? We have listed below various types of groups which are available for men to join. This list is not comprehensive, but will give you an idea of options. We have written a short description of the purpose and some positive advantages for each group, and have offered some suggestions and exercises for men's support groups and therapy groups.

Community Self-Help Groups

This family of groups centers around the use of "twelve-step" programs, and includes Alcoholics Anonymous (AA), Narcotics Anonymous (NA), Overeaters Anonymous (OA), and other spin-off groups, such as Adult Children of Alcoholics (ACOA). These groups focus on controlling addictions—alcohol, drugs, eating, gambling, sex, or others. They tend to be leaderless (no professional counselors) and geared toward group sharing and support. The groups are open to anyone (though some have specific rules, such as no smokers) who is willing to take the step of recognizing and accepting that he has a problem with addictions, and is deciding to do something about it. Many chapters of each organization operate in cities and towns, so in some locations, a person can find several meeting groups every day of the week.

Some men find these groups attractive because of anonymity (first names only) and the absence of confrontations. They are based on a twelve-step program which, in order to be effective, requires the acceptance that one is powerless over the addiction and that recovery can only take place with the help of a higher power. Each person is allowed to proceed toward recovery at his own rate. Experienced sponsors can be obtained to help the new member through the difficult periods of abstinence from the addiction. The combination of the twelve-step program with group support and the individual contact has provided a successful tool for a large number of people in giving up addictions.

Men's Clubs: Fraternities, Community Service, Religious

Men's clubs are a very diverse mixture of types and

people. Some are business related and membership is informal (Kiwanis, Rotary), while others are centered around community service and may involve initiation rites (Shrine Lodge). What draws men together in clubs depends on the goal of the group, whether it be business contacts, honoring former military service, church involvement, or commitment to charitable activities. Benefits of membership in such clubs include identification with the values and goals of the club, a sense of belonging, and camaraderie. These clubs focus more on values and commitment of the group than on individual personal growth.

Activity Groups

Activity groups organize men around shared participation in some task or ordeal. Athletic teams, investment groups, hobby clubs, and collectors' groups are all examples of men who get together to do something of shared interest. The focus is on enjoyment and success in the activity, as well as belonging to a group of like-minded individuals. Cohesion in these groups is usually strong, often strengthened by rituals with the activity—such as softball or gardening, which come along in the spring, or an annual show of cars, baseball cards, or guns—that rallies the group and centers their efforts. Activity groups allow for a channeling of competition, the use of skills or abilities, and a chance for passionate focus of one's talents and interests. Since many men work at jobs they find uninteresting and unfulfilling, these groups fill an important need in men's lives, the need to "do something" together with other men that is of great personal interest.

Men's Support Groups

Support groups were traditionally centered around a difficult life transition, such as divorce or death of a spouse. In the mid-1980s, however, a growing trend had developed among men from varied backgrounds, life experiences, religious preferences, ages, and sexual preferences, to gather together in order to share the pain of their lives, experience the support of a group of men, and learn more about what it means to themselves and other people to be a man.

These groups are forming in many places, such as churches, community centers, and universities. Sometimes the group structure is topic oriented, with a different subject each time, or a series on a particular subject, discussion centered and time limited (often five to ten weeks). Other groups are open-ended both with regard to content and time commitment. In these groups, time is shaped by concerns and needs brought to the group each meeting time. Support groups are becoming more popular as men are looking for others who share the desire to expand the limits of being male in our time, and many of these groups have had far-reaching success in helping men overcome fears about expressing emotions, being vulnerable with other men, and talking openly about their experience of being a man.

It is not unusual for these ongoing groups to offer occassional weekend retreats where well-known leaders in the men's movement come to speak and offer instruction and guidance for men in their personal lives.

Men's Therapy Groups

A therapy group bears some similarity to support groups. The focus is on introspection, search for self-knowledge, empathy and understanding for others, and support for change. The intent of a therapy group is to focus more intensely and directly on specific problematic areas in each man's life under the direction of a therapist. The goal of a men's therapy group is to look at current and past relationships in depth and work intently on change with direct intervention and guidance, whereas the support group focuses more on self-help with support from others.

Therapy groups tend to be smaller—four to eight men being the norm, rather than numbers of up to dozens or more for the support group—thus offering opportunity for more individual attention. These groups are led by a trained mental health professional who is paid for his time and expertise.

Men's therapy groups may be designed to concentrate on specific issues, such as parenting, friendships, sexual issues, or resolving family of origin problems; or their direction and goals may follow the lead of the problems brought by the members of the group. They may be "closed" or "open" in format. Closed groups are limited to a specific number of members and/or number of sessions. Open groups will usually be ongoing, or have members entering and leaving; thus the membership of the group will be changing over time.

There are benefits unique to men's therapy groups. Opportunities are provided to work through and resolve painful memories, wounds left over from old relationships, and to express feelings and thoughts in a safe, supportive environment. Interaction patterns of group members which block communication and alienate others are pointed out by the therapist in order to change destructive or isolating behaviors. The therapist's theory, training, and relative objectivity allow him to guide individual group members and the group as a whole to greater awareness and more healthy functioning.

Group Exercises

Here are some suggestions for exercises that can be used in men's support or therapy groups to help stimulate individual and group insight into many issues that men face.

Using Films and Videos

There are many good films portraying men dealing with the various topics we have discussed in this book. Watch a film "purposely." Then *write down* your reactions before you discuss the film with other people. The purpose of writing it down is to record, concretely and clearly, your own individual response to the powerful images portrayed in these films—to get you in touch with your own deeply personal experience. Then discuss the film with other people, with men or women. This is to have the sense of connecting what is deeply personal to you with what is felt and thought by other people. This is an exercise in connecting your inner world with the inner experience of other people.

This exercise can be used very profitably by men's groups. Get your men's group together, and rent a film. Then have a period of time (say, thirty minutes) afterward in which each man silently writes:

- His feelings about the characters and situations.
- His thoughts about the characters and situations.

- What memories he has from his own life that feel similar or are literally parallel to what happened in the film.

Then the group reconvenes and talks about what each of them has written. Some will wish to read what they have written and others will prefer to talk about the writing or about the experience of doing the exercise or other things. You might consider repeating this exercise several times, since different films deal with different topics and evoke varied reactions; films provide a great backdrop for discussion.

We have developed a brief list, with descriptions, of videos which emphasize aspects of the male experience. Use these videos and make your own additions.

The Great Santini—A powerful story of a son challenging his competitive father. Adolescent male friendship is also a central theme.

Wall Street—A story of an ambitious young man choosing an unethical mentor, and how he must ultimately reject the mentor, along with his greed and dishonesty.

Bull Durham—A baseball story which highlights the role of the mentor in shaping a raw recruit.

Stand by Me—Adolescent friendship is the basic theme of this story, especially how these friendships compensate for a lack of closeness with the father.

Stand and Deliver—A story set in a tough city school which focuses on how important a teacher can be in the lives of young men and women who have no positive models for learning and success. Learning is brought alive by the main character as something challenging and exciting. Based on a true story.

Dads—Three generations of males—grandfather, father

and son—all find something positive and valuable in their relationships with one another.

Men Don't Leave—A family tragically loses the father and has to cope with the emotional and other difficulties that arise. A fine film.

Jazz Singer—Neil Diamond stars in this remake of an old classic. He must break away from his father's legacy in order to find his own talents. In the process he finds his own identity and the love of a woman.

Indiana Jones and the Last Crusade—Entertaining action picture which highlights Indy's love–hate relationship with his father.

The Karate Kid—The role of the mentor is beautifully presented in this picture. The wise tutor teaches his pupil values and personal discipline along with skill.

The Flamingo Kid—Father and son break with each other over different values and choices in life. The son chooses a dishonest, corrupt mentor to follow. He ultimately must face his mistake, renounce his mentor, and reconcile with his father.

Star Wars (series)—Mentor–apprentice relationships and the dark father are at the crux of these films. Questions of good and evil, force and restraint, the use of shield and sword are all depicted, as well as the theme of reconciliation between father and son.

Dances with Wolves—This is an epic story which offers a view of "native" or "traditional" ways of life, the focus on ritual, rites of passage into manhood. We see the contrast of man resonating with nature, embodied in the Native Americans, over/against the egotistical and self-serving policies of expansionistic warfare practiced by cavalry soldiers.

Avalon—An emigrant family comes to America with hope for a better life. Family is the foundation upon which their dreams are built. A grandfather's profound role in the family is beautifully portrayed.

Platoon—Two styles of leadership, one bent on rampant, wanton destruction and another with a deeper humanity, are portrayed as ways of surviving the horrors of war. The themes of betrayal, competition, and war's crippling effect on the emotional lives of men are portrayed.

Birdy—Hopes, imagination, the dehumanization of an institutionalized society, and the saving role of profound friendships are portrayed in the lives of two young men.

When Harry Met Sally . . .—This is a model for the ultimate in "longer-term relationships." Harry and Sally spend a lifetime getting to know each other, finding their commitment to each other deepened with patience, time, and familiarity.

The Days of Wine and Roses—This great oldie demonstrates in a profound and articulate way the devastating effects of alcohol on a man's life.

Personal Philosophy Statement

Each man in the group writes a "personal philosophy" statement. The instructions for each person are as follows: Using the phrase "I believe . . . " state your views on issues of morals, ethics, the role of the family, politics, spirituality, the place of love, the afterlife, and the relationship between man and nature. For the purposes of this exercise, try to keep to a statement of your personal beliefs and away from any discussion of practical solutions to these questions. Write your best "sense" of your beliefs at this moment, even if you may not feel that you have final answers.

This exercise can be the focus of a *small* group discussion (no more than five people). One good format is to allow each person to read his personal philosophy statement or to focus on one issue per get-together and have each person read his perspective on that topic. The role of the other group members is not to debate or argue with the one presenting, but to make certain that they understand *what* he is presenting. To this end, group members can ask questions that help clarify the understanding.

If, for example, one person states, "I believe in reincarnation," the other group members would ask questions such as, "What kind of reincarnation—always as humans or with a hierarchy of development, or what? What do you think happens to the soul in between incarnations?" Reincarnation toward what purpose? What leads you to believe that way? Is this part of an overall view of the meaning of the universe? Again, the purpose of this exercise is not to argue or try to persuade him out of his view, but to help him understand his own view better.

One person should be nominated as "moderator" for the "class." It is his responsibility to see to it that the others help and support the individual in his quest to clarify and deepen his thinking, and to see to it that other people in the "class" stay out of attacking or trying to persuade the individual out of his philosophy. The purpose, once again, is to help men think for themselves.

Although men have some reputation for thinking and analyzing, many allow themselves to go "brain dead" after their formal education. This is the kind of adult discussion and development of philosophical thinking that was practiced in ancient times, and is a good practice to renew.

Let's think about what we believe, and think as carefully and thoroughly as we can. If we are going to presume to pass our view on to our sons and other younger men, we have the responsibility to think hard and long about what we "stand for" as individuals.

A Safe Exercise with Personal Boundaries for Group

Start with two men on the opposite sides of a room with a distance of at least ten feet between them. Have one *slowly* approach the other, keeping eye contact the whole time. Have him move to a distance that feels *comfortable*, whatever that distance is. It may be that he doesn't move at all, or it may be that he gets within two or three feet, or less, of the other man.

Have the one who moved describe what he thinks and feels, and particularly what he senses in his body. What is he aware of in his eyes, his arms, belly, legs, knees, and so on? Tightness, jitters, relaxed muscles, clenching, energy that makes him want to move, or a sense of frozenness?

Then have him move a little closer, just a little. If he was three feet away, have him move six inches closer than he was comfortable with before. Again have him describe what he thinks and feels and senses in his body.

Then move back to the "comfortable place," and step back a little, say a foot, and describe thoughts, feelings, and body sensations.

Now, have the one who moves stand still while the other one performs the same movements—to the "comfortable place," a step forward and then a step back away from the middle zone.

Re-form the group with both men back together with the others. Have both men talk about the experience, including the one who was stationary in each case. Ask others in the group to comment on their experience. Go around the room having others try the experiment. People describe everything from a "sense of fun and enjoyment" with this exercise to "sheer panic."

Most men, even ones with pretty strong resistance to any closeness or intimacy, describe this exercise as safe, and yet very "informational" in terms of their own personal boundaries, that is, the sense of closeness or distance from another man that feels "tolerable" to them.

This exercise can be modified successfully for kids' groups, classrooms, groups of men and women, and couples. In groups where there is already a pretty strong sense of safety and intimacy, the "leader" of the exercise can "push" the participants a little more, to try a little greater closeness or distance. But please keep the basic precept in this exercise, that of taking great care for each participant's comfort level.

Photograph Album

If it is available, go through old photograph albums of pictures taken by your family, with one or two other men. Ask them to comment on what they see. Look at the expressions on the faces and at the physical connections. How are people positioned with each other? Who is positioned near whom? Who generally stands or sits by whom? Pay particular attention to the men in the pictures. How do they look? Do they look particularly happy, sad, scared, dour, expressionless? Are there pictures of people showing physical attentiveness? Do the pictures appear spontaneous, lively, and energetic, or do they appear to be more wooden, stiff, lifeless? What information do you get about the men in your family and what seemed to be expected of them? How about men and women together? Men with children? Men with their own family of origin? These old photographs are real storehouses of information on relationships in your family.

Write down or tell aloud to others how you think things were in your father's relationship with his father; how they were or are with any brothers he had, or with any uncles he had. Then, write down how you think things are for you in each of these relationships. Bring what you wrote about your father and yourself back together and read them side-by-side. What do you notice?

Handshake

It is common for men to shake hands with one another. Here is an exercise to use in a men's group to promote personal awareness about this common experience. Here are the instructions:

Shake hands with someone else in the group; do it with awareness. Feel the other person's hand. Be aware of the grip, the strength or weakness in the other person's hand. How much pressure does the other person exert in the handshake? How much do you exert? How long does it last? Who stops first?

How do you feel about yourself shaking this person's hand? What do you feel toward him? Do you want more, would you like a hug instead? Or is that enough contact? Or too much? What are your thoughts about yourself and about him?

A Child's Toy

This exercise can be done alone or in a group. If it is done in a group, each individual should have some time alone to do the exercise (thirty minutes to an hour) and then everyone brought back together to discuss it.

Buy a child's toy, preferably something you remember playing with, that is moderately priced, does not run on batteries, and doesn't require much assembly. Can you remember playing with something simple and immediately usable? For example, a lot of kids had a rubber-band, wind-up glider plane. Whatever you can remember that you liked playing with, get it. If you don't remember something in particular, go into a toy store, and pick something simple and straightforward that you can play with in the next day or so. Take the toy home, put the phone on the answering machine, tell you partner or kids or anyone else who is likely to bother you to leave you alone for an hour or so, and play with the toy.

As you play with the toy, note your reactions. What feelings are you aware of? What memories or possibly resistance to remembering do you notice? Do you fight remembering yourself as a little boy? What was going on in your house when you were the age to play with a toy such as the one you have with you? Do you notice a sense of enjoyment, followed by sadness? Many people do, since it puts them in touch with what they have lost. What have you lost that you had in your childhood, or what do you notice that you never experienced in those days?

In the group, you may want to discuss the topics of enjoyment, pleasure, and playing. What is each man's experience of these? What feelings, thoughts, and memories did playing with the child's toy evoke in each man?

Courage

In your group, have each man do this exercise and then

gather together to discuss what thoughts, feelings, and memories came up during the exercise.

Write down your own inventory of courage, examples of courage that you have demonstrated. Measure "courage" by the standards that fit for *your context.* What takes courage for you, given your situation. Have you demonstrated courage in this way?

A Contract for Positive Change

Make a "contract" with someone else in the group that you will do something concrete and tangible to take care of yourself better. Make it *very* specific—the more specific the better. Set it up so it is very hard for you to cheat on it, and if you do, there will be consequences. Write it out and have the other person witness it in front of the whole group. For example:

Contract for Jogging Exercise

I will exercise two times a week, either Monday/Wednesday or Tuesday/Thursday. I will run two miles each time at a good even pace, enough to produce good aerobic effects. I will stretch out carefully before and have enough time for cool-down walking afterwards. I am giving Ted a signed check for one hundred dollars. If I don't fulfill this contract, he will make it out to the [name of organization that the person intensely dislikes], and submit it in my name.

Signed ____________________ Date____________________

Witnessed ____________________ Date____________________

Personal Myth

Much has been made of the function of myth in our lives. How about your own personal *pantheon of gods,* that is, the heroes and inspiring images of men that you have heard or seen in your life? The word *myth* comes from the Greek *muthos* which just means, simply, story. What stories charge you, draw you, have a power in your life? In a group of men, recall those stories and the effect they have had on you.

Robert tells about some stories in his life:

> I remember David and Goliath. That was an attractive story because I was a pipsqueak as a kid and thought that given courage and the right motivation I could "take out" a big guy if I wanted to.
>
> Now the Biblical David was great, but even better from my point of view was another David, Davey Crockett, portrayed by Fess Parker on TV. What I liked about him was that he was big, tough, wild and woolly, incredibly strong, and at the same time soft-spoken, calm, and very much in tune with nature, with the plants, animals, and seasons. He explored nature and hunted animals and got into fights sometimes, but was very moderated, very at home with himself.
>
> I don't know where my dream to be like him got off track, but I just now noticed, in thinking about it, how much this has happened. I have turned into a nervous, loud, grouchy, pushy person, totally out of touch with nature here in this tomb they call an office building. I am out of shape physically, tired, bored to death. God, I feel awful and not at home anywhere.

Father's Day

Do something for Father's Day, something different. Start a new tradition. Bring together fathers and sons, father figures and son figures, mentors and apprentices, grandfathers and grandsons, for a celebration. Ask men from each generation to speak up in support of men, in praise of men and boys they know.

Another idea: Send a card or letter to some older man who has been like a father to you. Tell him how he has influenced you, and thank him for what he has given you. Ask for his blessing for you now.

Suggested Readings

Bieber, I. *Homosexuality*. Jason Aronson: Northvale, New Jersey, 1988.
Lockhart, R. A. and Hillman, J. *Soul and Money*. Spring Publications: Dallas, Texas, 1982.
Napier, A. Y. *The Fragile Bond*. Harper and Row: New York, 1988.
Pittman, F. "Bringing Up Father," *Family Therapy Networker*, Vol. 12, no. 3, 1988, pp. 21–29.
Pittman, F. "The Masculine Mystique," *Family Therapy Networker*, Vol. 14, no. 3, 1990, pp. 46–53.
Weiss, P. *Modes of Being*. Southern Illinois University Press: Carbondale, Illinois, 1958.

Index